COMMUNICATING IN THE REAL WORLD

Developing Communication Skills for Business and the Professions

COMMUNICATING IN THE REAL WORLD

Developing Communication Skills for Business and the Professions

TERRENCE G. WILEY

HEIDE SPRUCK WRIGLEY

California State University, Long Beach

PRENTICE-HALL, INC., Englewood Cliffs, New Jersey 07632

Library of Congress Cataloging-in-Publication Data

WILEY, TERRENCE G.
    Communicating in the real world.

    "Designed to meet the needs of English as a Second
Language students and young adults"—Pref.
    1. Communication.   2. English language—Textbooks
for foreign speakers.   I. Wrigley, Heide Spruck.
II. Title.
P90.P477 1987   001.54   86–16985
ISBN 0-13-153974-4

Editorial/production supervision and
    interior design: **Patricia V. Amoroso**
Cover design: **George Cornell**
Manufacturing buyer: **Carol Bystrom**
Photo Research: **Christine Carey**
Photo Editor: **Lorinda Morris**

Printed in the United States of America

10 9 8 7 6 5 4 3 2 1

ISBN 0-13-153974-4 01

PRENTICE-HALL INTERNATIONAL (UK) LIMITED, *London*
PRENTICE-HALL OF AUSTRALIA PTY. LIMITED, *Sydney*
PRENTICE-HALL CANADA INC., *Toronto*
PRENTICE-HALL HISPANOAMERICANA, S.A., *Mexico City*
PRENTICE-HALL OF INDIA PRIVATE LIMITED, *New Delhi*
PRENTICE-HALL OF JAPAN, INC., *Tokyo*
PRENTICE-HALL OF SOUTHEAST ASIA PTE. LTD., *Singapore*
EDITORA PRENTICE-HALL DO BRASIL, LTDA., *Rio de Janeiro*

For Stephen B. Ross

CONTENTS

PREFACE

Communicating in the Real World is designed to meet the needs of English as a Second Language students and young adults who soon will be entering the world of work. The text is intended as a bridge between the theoretical world of schooling and the real world of employment.

Studies indicate that success in one's career is, to a great extent, tied to one's ability to communicate effectively. Knowledge of the language and its grammar is necessary but not sufficient for successful communication. It is not uncommon to hear frustrated second language learners, even after they have attained a considerable knowledge of the language, lament that their English is still not good enough. Their frustration may in part be related to an incomplete understanding of the rules of language, but it may also be related to an unfamiliarity with the cultural and social context in which communication occurs.

In such cases, the difficulties of the second language student are not entirely unlike those of the young native speaker of English who, entering the workplace for the first time, also fails to understand the rules of use, which are in large part determined by the social context of the organization. Both native and second language students must become attuned to the rules of use that are appropriate to the world of work and the subcultures of various companies.

Successful communication requires sensitivity to contextual cues; it involves problem perception and strategy formation. Consequently, this book is designed to help students to recognize important aspects of communication, to form communicative strategies, and to apply their communication skills.

Each chapter contains all or most of the following types of material:

1. Short readings related to a key aspect of communication in order to introduce or explain a concept.

2. Vocabulary exercises to ensure that students have the necessary terms to facilitate discussion.

3. Discussion questions to engage the student and to provide feedback to the instructor regarding the student's level of comprehension.

4. Problems for analysis and discussion wherein the student must deal analytically with general information as applied to specific situations.

5. Tips and suggestions, which are intended as guidelines but not strict prescriptions.

6. Simulations and role-playing exercises, which allow the students to try out what they have learned and to get constructive feedback from both the instructor and their peers.

To ground communication exercises in specific contexts, *Communicating in the Real World* uses numerous case studies and situations for analysis. Many of these are based upon actual situations. Every attempt has been made to give the text a real-world flavor based upon real-world experience. However, the classroom cannot substitute for outside experience.

Instructors should feel free to trust their own intuition and experience when discussing difficult problems and observing role plays. Since communication does not follow a script, the instructor (and the authors) realistically will not have all the answers. Often there is more than one way to handle a situation. Consequently, rather than looking for right versus wrong, the focus should be on what works more effectively versus what works less effectively. Student insight and experience should be solicited and used as a valuable complement to the expertise of the instructor.

ACKNOWLEDGMENTS

The development process for a book can often be a long one. We would like to acknowledge the influence of our former professor and colleague, Dr. Stephen B. Ross of California State University, Long Beach, who turned several of his seminars into testing grounds for communicative curriculum design. We are also greatly indebted to several hundred of our former students for whom much of the material was originally written as well as to dozens of employers who were consulted both prior to and during the writing of the manuscript. Special thanks also go to Karen Fox, Director of the American Language Program at California State University, Long Beach, who allowed the program to accommodate the field testing, and to Patricia Fullbright, who assisted in some of the field testing. Our thanks also go to Gordon Johnson of Prentice-Hall, who helped to facilitate communication with the editors. Last, we would like to thank the reviewers for their comments and the editors at Prentice-Hall for their assistance.

TERRENCE G. WILEY

HEIDE SPRUCK WRIGLEY

TO THE STUDENT

Many of you are planning to apply your skills in American business. Some of you will be employed by an American firm either in the United States or overseas, while others may plan to work for an international business that deals with American companies. To a certain extent, you are very well prepared. You probably have studied English for many years.

Over the years, you have accumulated a wealth of information about the English language, and some of you know more about rules of formal English grammar than the average native speaker. Yet many of you may feel inadequate when it comes to communicating your ideas in English, especially when that communication takes place not among friends but with people who may determine your professional future, that is, people in business, such as interviewers, clients, fellow workers, or supervisors.

As you become more and more familiar with the world outside of the classroom, you come to realize that real-world communication involves much more than grammar and vocabulary. For example, you may have no trouble at all making a grammatical sentence out of the words: *a raise/I/ want*. But knowing how to say, "I want a raise" is only one small part of asking for a promotion. Other factors that are much more significant come into play: factors such as whom to ask, when and where to ask, and how to ask. Should you march into the boss's office and say very forcefully, "I demand a raise" or should you humbly explain your financial problems and beg for an increase? Perhaps you have been on the job for only a few weeks and have not earned a right to ask for more money. As you can see, more is needed than merely knowing the English language.

Similarly, while a large vocabulary is a very worthwhile aid in communication, just knowing a large number of words will not help you in deciding what words to use under what circumstances. For example, on your first day at the office, your co-workers may casually introduce you to the janitor by saying, "Oh, by the way, this is our custodian, John." If you then respond with: "How do you do, John. I am so pleased to make your acquaintance. I have been looking forward to this moment *interminably*," you will sound rather ridiculous. John may even think that you are being sarcastic and are trying to make fun of him. He probably would have preferred that you simply say, "Glad to meet you, John." Thus even though both your grammar and vocabulary may be flawless, you will not be able communicate effectively if you are not aware of the rules of social conduct.

This text will concentrate on the rules of *social communication* instead of rules of grammar. It is designed as a simple cultural and linguistic guide to employment communication. Each chapter presents a different aspect of communication, and through examples and case studies you will be introduced to the types of problems and communicative challenges that employees face in the workplace. Through analysis and discussion of the cases, you will be able to develop the kinds of strategies that native speakers use to solve their communication problems on the job.

COMMUNICATING IN THE REAL WORLD

Developing Communication Skills for Business and the Professions

chapter 1

OVERVIEW:

"What's It All About?"

Michael Drummond/Picture Atlanta

INTRODUCTION

Usually we think of communication occurring only when we consciously intend to communicate. Actually, it often occurs even when we do not intend to communicate. For example, if you are tired and you keep yawning, you will communicate your fatigue. If you have an appointment and you show up late, you may unintentionally communicate that you are irresponsible, or that you do not take the appointment *very* seriously. You may have had a very good reason for being late, but unless you provide a good explanation, you may communicate a negative message.

What we communicate is called the *message*. As you can see from the examples above, the message does not even have to be a verbal message. A message is merely what we communicate. When we consciously try to communicate something, we may call it the *message intended*. What the other person experiences we may call the *message perceived*. In the case of coming late to an appointment, you may have a good reason for being late. You may not have intended any message, but if you do not explain the reasons for your being late, you might make an unfavorable impression. In other words, your actions can be perceived as having significance to other people even if that is not your intention.

Generally, the person sending the message is called the *sender*, whereas the person receiving the message is called the *receiver*. The message flows from the sender to the receiver. Communication also flows from the receiver back to the sender in the form of *feedback*.

Feedback is the receiver's reaction to the message. If you were to show up late for an appointment and the other person gave you a frown, that would be an example of nonverbal feedback. The following diagram represents a simplified model of what we have been discussing.

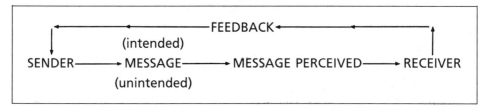

When a perceived message is different from an intended message, the result often is a breakdown in communication. Study the following example of a breakdown in communication:

Tuan: How about coming to my place for dinner Friday night?

Alan: Sure. Can I bring anything?

Tuan: (*puzzled*) Yes, bring as much as you like.

Alan: (*surprised*) Oh! Uh, gee, uh, how about some dessert and maybe something to drink?

In this case, both Tuan and Alan probably experienced some confusion. First, Tuan simply tried to make a friendly invitation. Alan's reply was culturally appropriate for an American but may have caught Tuan by surprise. Consequently, Tuan tried to reply with a polite agreement to Alan's offer to bring something, but his "bring as much as you like" was not an appropriate response. Thus, Alan was confused and stumbled in his answer.

As a result, the message that Alan intended was one for which Tuan was not prepared. Conversely, the message that Tuan communicated was not one for which Alan was prepared. Communication involves more than just grammar and vocabulary; it involves knowledge of the culture and awareness of social rules as well. In this chapter we will begin to look at some of the major factors that affect and influence our ability to communicate effectively, especially our ability to communicate effectively in the workplace.

VOCABULARY CHECK

Match the following terms with the explanation below that best explains the term or concept.

_____ a. intend

_____ b. message

_____ c. verbal

_____ d. message intended

_____ e. message perceived

_____ f. significance

_____ g. sender

_____ h. receiver

_____ i. feedback

_____ j. breakdown in communication

1. meaning
2. signals that the receiver communicates to the sender
3. the message as interpreted by the receiver

4. spoken

5. hope or try to do

6. one who transmits a message

7. the message that you try to communicate

8. one who gets a message

9. that which results when a perceived message is different from an intended message

10. what one communicates consciously or unconsciously

QUESTIONS FOR DISCUSSION

1. Do we only communicate what we intend to communicate? Explain and give examples.

2. What is the difference between "message perceived" and "message intended"? Explain.

3. What is the relationship between sender and receiver? Explain.

4. What do we mean by feedback? Explain.

5. How did the breakdown in communication occur in the example given?

KEY COMMUNICATION FACTORS

In order to cope with the difficult process of communicating our ideas effectively, we need to develop strategies for determining how to respond in different situations. We need to know not only what to say (if anything at all), but when to say it, who to say it to, and perhaps most important of all, how to say it. One strategy for making these decisions is to look at the key communication factors that are involved in sending and receiving a message. We can determine these factors by asking ourselves a series of questions and using the answers to decide how to react.

Communication Factor 1: The Language Function

Key Question: What is the purpose of the interaction?

Problem

Sometimes we understand all the words in a statement or a question, yet we are still unsure of the message that the other person is sending.

Laimute E. Druskis

Example

When your boss asks you: "Would you mind straightening out that report you gave me? There are a number of errors in the data," you may not be sure how to respond. You may not be certain whether your boss is asking you a personal favor (in which case you could say either yes or no to his request), or whether he is telling you what to do (in which case you do not have much of a choice).

You cannot react appropriately until you have analyzed the situation and determined, either consciously or unconsciously, what your boss really meant by his question. Determining the purpose of an interaction is called determining the *language function.*

Communication Factor 2: Domain

Key Question: What rights and responsibilities do I have in this area?

Problem

In any job, it may be difficult to decide what a person's rights and responsibilities are.

Example

You may not know how to respond when the company representative asks you during a job interview whether you have any children. You may think that this is a personal question that has nothing to do with your professional qualifications. You may even feel that the question is discriminatory and cannot be asked legally.

Before you decide how to react to such a question, you should know what your rights are. After you have determined these rights, you still have the option of either fighting the situation or going along to maintain peace. The area to which a particular subject belongs is called *domain*.

Communication Factor 3: Register Use

Key Question: Whom am I talking to?

Problem

Sometimes we are not sure of how to respond because we are not certain of our place or status in the organization.

Example

You may know a great number of slang terms and colloquialisms, such as, "Hey, don't worry. Take it easy," but you are not sure whether it would be all right to use these expressions with those who are above you in the organization (your superiors), or whether you would offend them. Similarly, if you are a new boss, you may not be sure how to address your American subordinates, that is, the people who work for you. Should you call them by their first name or their last name? You may ask yourself if it is a good idea to get involved in their personal problems, or if you should assume that their life outside of the office has nothing to do with their job. Similarly, you may sometimes wonder what the best way may be to handle those that are on the same level as you (your co-workers or your peers). For example, should you tell a fellow employee when he or she is making a mistake, or should you mind your own business? If you do decide to bring it up, what might be the most tactful way?

You will not be able to decide what to say to whom or in what manner until you have determined where you stand in relation to the other people. Changing your language according to the relative status of the speakers is called *register use*.

Communication Factor 4: Degree of Urgency

Key Question: How important is the message?

Problem

Every once in a while we are suddenly faced with an unusual problem that may demand immediate attention.

Example

Your child calls you in the middle of the afternoon to inform you that she has missed the school bus and does not have a ride back home. You are in the middle of a conversation with your boss, and you are not sure what to do. Should you leave to get your child immediately, or do you have time to consider alternatives? Should you rush out of the office and explain the problem later, or would it be better to finish the conversation?

In order to make that decision, you need to evaluate the circumstances to determine whether you are dealing with a true emergency or a situation that can be dealt with in a routine manner. The relative importance of the message is called _degree of urgency_.

Communication Factor 5: Style and Attitude

Key Question: How do I come across?

Problem

Sometimes it is difficult to see ourselves as others see us, and our perception of ourselves may not be shared by those around us.

Example

You may be a person who thinks it is extremely important to allow people to save face no matter what the situation. Therefore, you seldom admit that you do not understand something or that you have made a mistake because you do not want to look foolish in the eyes of those that work with you. Similarly, you may not like to embarrass others, so you seldom disagree with anyone's decision even though you may be sure the person is making a mistake.

To make sure others see you as the kind of person that you are, it is important to check your perception of yourself with the image you project to others. The image that you project is called your _style and attitude_.

VOCABULARY CHECK

Fill in the blank spaces in the sentences below with the appropriate words from the following list. Not all these words will be used.

factor	colloquialism
strategy	superior
language function	subordinate
interaction	routine

> data   degree of urgency
> register use   attitude
> status   domain

1. A person who works below you in an organization is called your

   _____ .

2. _____ is your area of responsibility or authority.

3. The way you feel about your work is your _____ .

4. The relative importance of a message refers to its

   _____ .

5. _____ refers to a plan of action.

6. An important part or element is called a(n)

   _____ .

7. A conversation or communication between people is called a(n)

   _____ .

8. _____ refers to an informal expression.

9. Something that is usual and repetitive is a(n)

   _____ .

10. _____ refers to information collected (often numbers or figures).

QUESTIONS FOR DISCUSSION

1. When we say we are trying to determine the language function, what are we trying to determine?

2. What communication factor do you have to keep in mind when you are trying to communicate with someone whose position is above yours?

3. What communication factor comes into play when an interviewer asks you whether or not you are planning to get married?

4. What are you trying to decide when you decide on the degree of urgency? Explain.

5. What question do you ask yourself when you are trying to determine your style and attitude?

APPROPRIATENESS

People who understand such factors as register use or style are able to respond appropriately in a variety of situations. In other words, they are able to match their response to the situation in question. People who speak without analyzing the situation first, however, more often run into trouble.

For example, the worker who demands to be given overtime by telling his boss: "You have to give me overtime. I need the money" is acting inappropriately since we generally do not have the right to be given overtime. However, the worker who requests overtime by saying: "I am available to work extra hours any time you need me. I'd appreciate it if I could get some extra hours" is acting within his rights and thus shows a good sense of appropriateness.

People who know how to communicate effectively have learned how to be flexible and vary their style. The following strategies show how you can modify your language and adjust your style by taking key communication factors into account.

TIPS FOR IMPROVING YOUR ABILITY TO COMMUNICATE

1. Determine the Purpose of a Statement or the Language Function

If your boss asks you, "How many times did we meet with Mr. Smith last month?" you can assume that the purpose of the question is to get information. However, if your boss asks you, "How many times must I tell you not to take a late lunch?" he or she is probably not looking for information, but rather expressing impatience with your refusal to follow company rules.

2. Determine the Proper Domain

If as a manager you feel that members of your staff dress inappropriately for work, you have the right to inform them that the company expects its employees to dress in a professional manner (for example, no shorts or T-shirts). However, if you run into some of your employees at the beach and are shocked by the skimpy bathing suits they are wearing, you do not have the right to criticize them for their immodesty.

3. Determine the Appropriate Register

If a friend asks why you are behind in your work once again, it is all right to tell the friend that you would rather not talk about it. However, the same response would be considered inappropriate if your *boss* asked you the same question.

4. Determine the Proper Degree of Urgency

If as a supervisor you ask your staff to stay late to compile information for a report that is due the following day, most employees will consider your request justified. However, if you regularly ask your staff to stay late without explaining the reason, most of your employees will resent your request.

AT&T Co. Photo Center

5. Develop a Friendly Style

If your colleagues are planning a farewell party for a co-worker and ask you if you would like to join the party and contribute money toward a gift, and you say, "No" and nothing more, they may feel that you do not care about the people you work with. However, if you explain that your financial situation is rather tight that month and the most you can contribute is a dollar or so, your co-workers will probably understand your reasons.

QUESTIONS FOR DISCUSSION

1. Why is the worker who says, "You have to give me overtime" acting inappropriately?

2. What kind of answer is your boss expecting when he asks you, "How many times do I have to tell you to get back from lunch on time?"

3. What reaction might your friends show if you told them you don't want to talk about why you are not getting your work done? What would your boss's reaction be?

4. Under what circumstances are employees usually willing to stay late and do extra work? Explain.

5. Imagine that your co-workers are asking you whether you would like to join them for a farewell party for one of the other employees. What impression will you make if you turn down their invitation by simply saying, "No" and nothing more?

6. Why is it inappropriate for a supervisor to criticize his or her employees for the kind of clothes they are wearing at the beach? Would the situation be different if it involved a beach party sponsored (given) by the company? Explain your opinion.

PROBLEMS FOR ANALYSIS AND DISCUSSION

Directions: *Each of the following cases involves one or more of the key communication factors discussed. Read the cases carefully and answer the questions that follow.*

Case 1

Ms. Sittner works as a clerk in a shipping company. She is getting married soon, so she has been meeting with her girlfriends during her lunch hour to discuss the wedding plans. Her official lunch hour is from twelve o'clock to one o'clock, but sometimes the conversations take longer than an hour and she gets back to work late.

One day as Ms. Sittner leaves for lunch, her boss stops her in the hall and asks her, "If it's not too much trouble, do you think you can be back by one o'clock for a change?"

In your opinion, why did Ms. Sittner's boss stop her? What was the purpose of his question? Circle the best answer.

Marc Anderson

_____ a. He is telling Ms. Sittner that he has noticed she has been taking long lunch hours, and he expects her to be on time from now on. He is *criticizing* her behavior.

_____ b. He is asking Ms. Sittner if she would mind coming back after an hour. If she thinks the discussion will take longer, she can tell him. He is just *asking for information*.

_____ c. He is *making a request* (asking a favor of her). He is asking her to come back on time just this one day because he needs her for something.

_____ d. He is just *teasing* her. He is giving her a hard time because he likes her. Ms. Sittner should not take his question seriously.

_____ e. Other (explain).

DISCUSSION

If you were Ms. Sittner, how would you react to the boss's question?

Get together in small groups and discuss and compare your answers. See if you can agree on what the boss was trying to tell Ms. Sittner. Then decide as a group what might be the best way for Ms. Sittner to react. Be ready to explain your decisions to the rest of the class. Write the group's answer in the space below. What was the boss's purpose?

Case 2

John Clark is a technician for an electronics company. His supervisor is Mr. Garcia. One afternoon the phone rings and Mr. Garcia's wife is on the line. John explains to her that her husband is in a budget meeting. Mrs. Garcia asks John to tell her husband to please pick up the children from their soccer practice at 5:30 P.M. It is 1:00 P.M. when the call comes in.

In your opinion, how should John handle the situation? Circle the best answer. If you can think of an additional possibility, write it in the space provided.

———— a. John should interrupt the meeting and give his boss the message immediately. If he waits, he might get involved in something else and forget; then both his boss and his boss's wife might be angry with him.

———— b. John should not interrupt the meeting. The message is not all that urgent and it can wait until after the meeting is over. Remembering to pick up the children does not qualify as an emergency.

———— c. John should forget that he ever received that phone call. The message has nothing to do with the job John is supposed to do. If Mrs. Garcia wants to leave personal messages, she should call back and talk to the secretary.

———— d. Other (explain).

DISCUSSION

If you were John, what would you say to Mr. Garcia when you saw him?

Break into small groups and discuss what each of you thought John should do. Try to determine how John's boss might react in each case. Then try to come to an agreement on what John should do or say. Write the group's answer in the space provided.

FROM THEORY TO PRACTICE: TRYING IT ON YOUR OWN

Individual Responses

Respond to the following cases in the way you think is most appropriate. Write down both what you would do and what you would say under the circumstances.

1. Your co-workers invite you to go to lunch with them. You have known most of them for a long time, and you are good friends with them. You have only five dollars in your wallet, not enough to pay for lunch at the restaurant they are suggesting. How would you handle the situation?

2. Your boss has asked you if he can borrow your calculator for a few minutes so that he can balance his checkbook. You loan him your calculator, but your boss has not returned it by the time you are ready to go home. How would you handle the situation?

3. You are trying to get some important work done, but the other people in the office are making so much noise, laughing and telling jokes, that it is very difficult for you to concentrate. How would you handle the situation?

4. A young woman who works for you has come to work late five days in a row. You do not know what her problem is. How would you handle the situation?

5. One of your co-workers is telling you: "Boy, I don't know what to do. I gained five pounds last week. I am getting fatter by the minute, and pretty soon I won't be able to fit into my clothes." How would you react to his statement?

6. A co-worker is about to step into the boss's office to ask for a favor. You know for a fact that the boss is in a very bad mood because the company has just lost a major contract. Would you warn your co-worker? If so, what would you say?

7. You are working as a clerk/typist in a small company. One day your boss wants you to go to the store to get him some cigarettes. How would you handle the situation?

8. Your boss is in an important meeting. You take a call from his wife, who is stranded on the highway and needs him to pick her up. How would you handle the situation?

9. You are using the company phone to make a personal call. You are in the middle of an interesting conversation when your boss asks you how much longer you plan to be on the phone. How would you respond?

10. You have been spending so much time thinking and talking about the vacation you are planning to take that you have gotten behind in your work. One day your boss asks you why you have not completed your project. How would you respond?

Role Playing

With another person, choose several of the cases from the exercise above. Role-play the situation, filling in the details as you go along. Remember that you will need to adapt your responses to your partner's reaction.

Group Discussion

Compare the way you analyzed each case with the way others interpreted the situation. Then through class discussions decide which solutions might be the most effective.

chapter 2

LANGUAGE FUNCTIONS:

What Are You Trying to Say?

Firestone News Service

INTRODUCTION

As you have seen in chapter 1, communication involves more than a knowledge of the grammar and the vocabulary of a language; it involves also, and perhaps most importantly, an awareness of how we use language in a social context. If you want to learn to communicate effectively, you must first realize that all communication takes place for a purpose. At work your purpose may have to do with a technical aspect of your work, as when you ask for or give information, or it may involve one of the social aspects of work such as asking your co-workers a favor or thanking them for the help they have given you. The purpose of the message you want to communicate is called the *language function*. The major work-related language functions can be broken down into five basic categories. These are: (1) exchanging information, (2) making requests, (3) persuading others to do what we want, (4) evaluating, and (5) expressing feelings, opinions, and attitudes.

These functions can be further divided into smaller components; the following is a list of the most common functions used at work:

> asking for and giving information
> asking for clarification
> elaborating
> double-checking information
> showing comprehension or lack of comprehension
> expressing concern or dissatisfaction
> showing sympathy
> responding to criticism
> giving reasons
> apologizing
> making excuses
> interrupting
> asking for permission
> offering help
> making requests
> making suggestions
> admitting fault
> showing enthusiasm
> explaining a problem

As you know, the message you want to send can be expressed either verbally or nonverbally. Thus any function can be expressed either through words or through body movements and gestures. Often a strong point can be made through silence.

In this chapter you will get practice in understanding various language functions, and you will learn how to express those functions in the most effective ways in English.

VOCABULARY CHECK

Match the following terms with the numbered phrase below that best explains the term or concept:

_____ a. asking for clarification

_____ b. elaborating

_____ c. double-checking information

_____ d. expressing dissatisfaction

_____ e. showing lack of comprehension

_____ f. responding to criticism

_____ g. apologizing

_____ h. making requests

_____ i. making suggestions

_____ j. admitting fault

1. saying that you have made a mistake; not trying to cover up your errors
2. showing that you are unhappy with something; explaining that things are not going well
3. giving further explanations
4. reacting to someone's negative comments about you
5. saying that you are sorry
6. proposing different possibilities
7. asking that something be made clearer or explained further
8. showing that you have not understood; showing that you don't know what to do
9. checking to make sure that you have understood what was said and what you were supposed to do
10. asking for a favor; asking that you be allowed to do something

QUESTIONS FOR DISCUSSION

1. What factors does communication involve?

2. Name one of the first things you must realize if you want to communicate effectively.

3. What may be your purpose in communicating when you are involved in the technical aspect of your work?

4. What may be your purpose in communicating when you are involved in the social aspect of your work?

5. Name the five basic categories of language functions.

6. Assume that you have left at home important information that your boss needs. Which functions would you use in explaining the problem to her or him?

COMMON LANGUAGE FUNCTIONS

Most language functions can be expressed in a number of standard forms that are easily recognized. For example, a person who says, "I'm sorry" is most likely trying to apologize, and someone who says, "I'm not sure what you mean by that" is expressing incomprehension and possibly asking for clarification. Most of the time there is more than one way to express a particular function. The speaker chooses a form that fits the situation and that best expresses his or her intentions. For example, if you need to borrow someone's calculator to add up a number of figures, you can select a number of expressions to make your request. You could say:

    a. Can I borrow your calculator for a minute?

       or

    b. Let me have your calculator, will you?

       or

    c. Would it be all right if I borrowed your calculator for a minute?

Which form you would choose would depend on the circumstances. For instance, you would probably not use form b with your boss, because the expression is rather informal. So even though a number of different forms can be used to express the same function, the expressions are not necessarily interchangeable. Each form gives an indication of how formal the situation is and how familiar you are with the other speaker, and if you

Teri Leigh Stratford

fail to recognize the differences, you will make an unfavorable impression on the people around you.

Following is a partial list of language functions and some common ways used to express those functions. As you go through the list, try to determine under which circumstances each expression might appropriately be used.

1. **Expressing lack of comprehension**

   a. I have no idea what you are talking about.

   b. I'm sorry; I don't quite understand what you are saying.

   c. I can't understand what you mean.

2. **Asking for clarification/double-checking**

   a. How many copies did you say you needed?

   b. Now tell me again. How many copies was that?

   c. That was thirty copies, right?

3. **Making a suggestion**

   a. Maybe we could talk about it over lunch.

   b. Why don't we talk about it over lunch?

   c. Let's talk about it over lunch, OK?

4. **Making an offer**

   a. Do you want me to stay late and finish?

   b. Why don't I stay late and finish up?

   c. I guess I could stay late and finish up.

5. **Expressing disagreement**

   a. I don't think that's right.

   b. I'm afraid I see things differently.

   c. That's the dumbest idea I have ever heard.

6. **Expressing dissatisfaction**

   a. I'm afraid I won't be able to finish all of this work on time.

   b. How am I supposed to finish all of this work? It's impossible.

   c. You have given me too much work. I need more time.

7. **Responding to criticism**

   a. I have not been late three days in a row. I was here on time Wednesday.

   b. I'm very sorry. I have had a lot of problems lately. I'll be on time from now on.

   c. There are a lot of other people here who don't show up on time. Why are you picking on me?

8. **Showing sympathy**

   a. I'm sorry that you are having problems at home. So just try to do the best you can here.

   b. I'm sorry that your father is sick. Is there anything I can do to help?

   c. I'm sorry about your father.

MATCHING EXPRESSIONS AND FUNCTIONS

Match the expressions (a–f) with the numbered functions listed above them. Be careful to note the social relationship. Note that social relationships often *affect what we say and how we say it. Social relationships will be discussed further in chapter 4, "Register Use."*

1. expressing sympathy
2. expressing disagreement
3. making a suggestion
4. expressing criticism
5. making an offer
6. responding to criticism/apologizing

_____ a. I'm sorry; I didn't mean to do that. I promise you it won't happen again.
Relationship: talking to a manager or other superior

_____ b. You must feel terrible. I wish there were something I could do.
Relationship: talking to a friend or a subordinate

_____ c. Why don't we all chip in and send some flowers.
Relationship: friend (peer) or subordinate

_____ d. I'm sorry, but you will just have to learn to work a little faster.
Relationship: manager to subordinate

_____ e. Why don't I stay after work for a few minutes and show you how to fill out those forms.
Relationship: friend, peer, boss to subordinate

_____ f. I don't quite see things the same way.
Relationship: peer, subordinate to boss, superior to subordinate

PROBLEMS FOR ANALYSIS AND DISCUSSION

Major problems can occur when people do not agree on how a particular function should be expressed or how a particular response should be interpreted. At work the ability to show *comprehension* (or lack thereof) is especially critical if miscommunication is to be avoided.

Study the following case and try to determine what went wrong. Then answer the questions that follow.

Courtesy of IBM

Case 1

Ms. Vo was an employee in a small accounting firm. After she had worked there for a while, her boss, Mr. Miller, decided that she was ready to learn to operate the computer. He took Ms. Vo to the terminal and showed her what to do. He explained to her what keys she needed to press to get on the computer and what steps she had to perform to enter the necessary information. He also told her what to do in case she made a mistake. As Mr. Miller went through his explanations, Ms. Vo realized that her boss was speaking much too fast for her to understand all the details. Nevertheless, she kept nodding her head while he was talking to let him know that she was listening. When Mr. Miller got to the end of his explanation, he asked Ms. Vo if she had any questions. Ms. Vo, who had no idea what questions she could possibly ask, said, "No." Mr. Miller assumed that he had made himself clear and left, convinced that his new employee knew exactly what to do; otherwise, she would certainly have asked him to repeat his instructions. Ms. Vo, on the other hand, was shocked to see her boss walk away without repeating what he wanted her to do. Didn't he realize that she had barely understood anything of what he had told her?

Briefly answer the following questions.

1. In the case above, Ms. Vo kept nodding her head while Mr. Miller was talking. In your opinion, what was she trying to tell Mr. Miller? How did Mr. Miller interpret Ms. Vo's nodding? What did he think? Why did Mr. Miller ask Ms. Vo if she had any questions? What was he trying to find out?

2. Why did Ms. Vo say that she didn't have any questions? What was she trying to tell her boss?

3. How did the misunderstanding occur? What mistake did Mr. Miller make? What mistake did Ms. Vo make? What should they have done differently?

4. Who bears greater responsibility for the breakdown in communication, Ms. Vo or Mr. Miller?

5. What could Ms. Vo have done to correct the situation after Mr. Miller walked off?

TIPS FOR AVOIDING MISCOMMUNICATION

Miscommunication of the type that Ms. Vo and Mr. Miller were experiencing is quite common and can be very frustrating to all concerned. As an employee, you will constantly be given instructions, and unless you have understood all directions clearly, you will not be able to do your job effectively. Because tasks that are performed incorrectly may cost a company thousands of dollars in wasted time or broken equipment, it is extremely important that you have understood every detail before beginning to work on a new project. To avoid major misunderstandings and potential problems, keep the following tips in mind.

Signal When You Don't Understand

When responding to instructions, show your lack of understanding as soon as possible; don't hope that you will figure out what to do eventually; communicate that you have trouble understanding as soon as you realize you are not sure what the other person wants you to do; don't wait until someone has completed a fifteen-minute explanation and then say, "I beg your pardon?" This may make the other person feel that he has wasted his time.

Send Either Verbal or Nonverbal Messages

You can express your lack of comprehension either verbally by interrupting the speaker or nonverbally by frowning or looking confused. If you don't know how to look confused "in English," you may be much better off saying something like, "Excuse me?" or "I'm sorry?" It is important to say both phrases with a rising intonation so that it is clear you are expressing lack of understanding and not apologizing for something you have done. Listen to your instructor model the difference and practice the right tone with your friends.

Ask That Critical Information Be Repeated

If you think that you have understood the information but you are not 100 percent sure, ask the other person to repeat the directions or give further explanations. Try to be as specific as possible when explaining where you are having problems. For example, Ms. Vo could have said, "I think I remember how to get started, but I am not sure what to do when I've made a mistake and what to do when I'm finished."

Ask for Clarification

If you have understood most of what your boss has told you but you are still not sure what to do, ask for clarification. In other words, find out exactly what is expected of you. You may say, "I'm sorry, I'm not sure what you want me to do" or something similar. This also holds true if your boss is using terms that you are unfamiliar with. Remember, however, that it is possible to understand a message without knowing the meaning of every single word, so try to relax and grasp the essential points.

Double-Check and Ask for Feedback

Even if you think you have understood the directions that you have been given, repeat the information in order to be sure that there is no misunderstanding. This is especially important when you are dealing with words that are easily confused. For example, if you are being told to make nineteen copies of a document, you might say something like, "That's nineteen, one-nine, right?" to make sure you don't end up making ninety copies instead. Similarly, if you are doing a job for the first time, it is a good idea to have a knowledgeable person look it over so that you won't repeat any mistakes you might have made. Double-checking is especially important for telephone conversations.

Don't Worry About Saving Face

Remember, no one expects you to be perfect, but bosses do expect you to let them know if you have trouble. Your boss knows that it is much cheaper and less time-consuming to repeat directions and prevent errors than to fix mistakes after they have occurred.

Be Honest and Don't Try to Cover Up Mistakes

If you have made a mistake that you cannot or should not correct yourself, make sure you let your boss know immediately. Don't try to cover up your mistakes hoping they will stay hidden. They won't. Try to imagine how foolish and embarrassed you will feel when your supervisor finds out the truth. Most supervisors feel that making mistakes is natural but that trying to hide a mistake is being dishonest and irresponsible.

COMBINING FUNCTIONS

Obviously, functions do not occur in isolation. Questions are usually followed by answers, unclear directions by requests for clarification, bad news by expressions of sympathy, and good news by expressions of excitement. Offers of help are either accepted or politely rejected, and requests are either denied, granted, or put off until a later date ("Let me think about it"). To allow for human feelings and other special considerations, functions are often extended beyond the essential information. For example, an employee who asks a special favor of his boss would do well to give a short explanation of his problem and provide a reason as to why he is making the request. Similarly, a boss who is concerned about keeping his or her employees happy would not turn down a legitimate request without giving an explanation as to why permission cannot be granted. Adding reasons and providing further information that allows the other person to understand the situation are called *elaborating*. Elaborating is often necessary to keep conversations running smoothly and the atmosphere friendly.

Study the following case and note what functions are used to elaborate beyond the basic information. Then answer the questions that follow.

Case 2: "Let Me Tell You About My Situation"

Ms. Ibrahim: Excuse me, Mr. Winting. Could I talk to you a minute? (*request for permission to interrupt*)

AT&T Co. Photo Center

Mr. Winting: Sure, go ahead. (*permission given*)

Ms. Ibrahim: I have a problem. My parents are arriving from Kuwait tomorrow and they need to be picked up from the airport because they don't speak any English. (*explanation of problem; reason for request*) I would like to take a personal holiday so that I will be able to get them. (*request for permission to take the day off*) I am all caught up on my work, and Ms. Sindaha knows what to do if there are problems. (*assurance that work will not be interrupted because of personal problems*)

Mr. Winting: Well, as you know, we have a contract due in a few days, and I really could use every person in the office in case any last-minute problems come up. (*stalling; appeal for the other person to withdraw her request*)

Ms. Ibrahim: I would ask my husband, but he is out of town on a business trip. (*explanation as to why request is not withdrawn*)

Mr. Winting: I'll tell you what, what time are your parents scheduled to come in? (*requesting further information; setting things up*)

Ms. Ibrahim: One-thirty. (*responding*)

Mr. Winting: Why don't you come to work in the morning and then take off the afternoon to take care of your parents. (*reasonable compromise; partial granting of request*)

Ms. Ibrahim: I suppose that would work. Thank you. (*acceptance of compromise*)

Mr. Winting: I'm sorry I can't let you have the whole day off, but we really need people available. (*apology and reason why permission was not granted as requested*)

Ms. Ibrahim: I understand. Thank you. (*acceptance of apology and expression of gratitude*)

Briefly answer the following questions.

1. What would the conversation sound like if neither Ms. Ibrahim nor Mr. Winting gave reasons and used elaboration? Write the dialogue.

2. What impression would the speakers have of each other if only the basic dialogue took place? What would Mr. Winting think of Ms. Ibrahim and vice-versa?

MAKING REQUESTS AND ASKING FOR PERMISSION

As the interaction between Ms. Ibrahim and Mr. Winting showed, asking for permission can be difficult. On the one hand, an employee has rights that cannot be taken away by an employer (minimum wage, a safe working environment, guaranteed vacation time). On the other hand, there are privileges that can be granted or denied depending on the situation (or the mood of the person in charge). Such privileges may include personal time off without pay, special assignments, or vacations at a specific time. Thus, while you may and should demand to be given the rights guaranteed in your contract, you can only *request* things that are considered privileges. Consequently, it is a good idea to think carefully before you ask for permission so that you can present your request in the best possible light and maximize your chances of success.

TIPS FOR MAKING REQUESTS AND ASKING PERMISSION

Look at the Overall Situation

Remember that your boss has to make decisions that affect the entire company. He needs to keep production going and must maintain a positive atmosphere among his employees. Requests that cost the company extra money, interfere with established work patterns, or are likely to cause resentment among the rest of the employees will surely be denied. Unless you can assure your supervisor that the granting of your request will not disrupt the workings of the rest of the department, it is better not even to ask.

Don't Fabricate (Invent) Emergencies

Most supervisors are willing to grant an occasional request as long as it does not interfere with the work being done. This is especially true if a request is prompted by an emergency situation such as the death of a family member or the illness of a child. However, since there is an average number of emergencies that each employee is supposed to encounter, it is not a good idea to fabricate an emergency where none exists. If you do, then when a truly urgent situation does arise, your special request may be denied because your boss may feel that you have had your share of emergencies for the month.

Besides, if you try to make up a story instead of telling the truth, there is always a chance that you will be found out and look both dishonest and stupid. We are reminded of the young man who, when filling out a request form for a day off that was two months away, gave as his reason: "I have to go to a funeral." Needless to say, his request was denied.

Keep a Low Profile

If you are lucky enough to be granted a special privilege, don't "flaunt" it. That is, don't walk around work announcing to everyone that your boss has given you the afternoon off so that you can meet a long-lost friend who will be in town only one day. Similarly, if your request has been denied, accept the fact gracefully and don't complain to everyone about what a slave driver the supervisor is.

GIVING REASONS AND MAKING EXCUSES

When we make a request or ask for permission, we are often expected to *explain why* we need special treatment. Giving reasons is one of the most frequently used functions at work. Many people try to avoid giving reasons because they are afraid they will get into trouble, or they may feel that their reasons are personal and no one's business but their own. Not giving any reasons may sometimes be a personal privilege, but in work-related matters your boss expects to know why things are happening: He has a right to know why you will need the day off, why you need more time to finish a project, why you feel you deserve a raise, or why you did not complete your job in a manner expected of you. As far as the social aspect of your work is concerned, your co-workers may feel that you owe them an explanation when you decide to change established patterns, act less friendly than usual, turn down an invitation, or refuse to participate in a group activity. While you need not go into endless details about your reasons, you should provide explanations whenever necessary so that others can understand you and your situation. Keep in mind, however, that sometimes co-workers ask questions about areas that are really none of their business. In such cases, a humorous response often works best.

PROBLEMS FOR ANALYSIS AND DISCUSSION:
Giving Reasons and Making Excuses

Following is a list of questions you might hear at work. Study the situations and provide either logical reasons or plausible excuses (excuses that make sense) for each.

1. A co-worker says: "You have been in this country for quite a while now. How come you still have trouble with your English?" What answer would you give if your boss asked that question? Explain.

2. A co-worker says: "I know you are new in this country, so my wife and I would like to invite you to come to church with us on Sunday." If you were not a Christian or did not wish to go, what would you say? What would your answer be if your boss asked that question? Explain.

3. A co-worker says: "How come you smoke so much? Don't you know that it's bad for your health?" Explain what you would say.

4. A co-worker says: "How come you don't want to join us for a few drinks after work? I'm sure you would have a good time." If you don't drink, what would you say? Explain.

5. Your boss says: "Do you realize that you have come in late to work three times this week?" Explain how you would respond.

6. A co-worker says: "How come your people have so many children?" What would you say? Explain.

7. A co-worker says: "I'll be having a cosmetics party at my house this Friday night. You won't have to buy anything if you don't want to, but I would like you to come." Explain how you would respond.

8. Your boss says: "Since you have just joined the company, my wife and I would like to have you and your wife over for dinner sometime soon." What would you say? Explain.

9. A co-worker says: "You seem to be such an interesting person. Why don't we go out sometime?" What would your answer be if your married boss asked you the same question? Explain.

10. A co-worker says: "Why did you come to this country?" How would you respond? Explain.

FROM THEORY TO PRACTICE: TRYING IT ON YOUR OWN

Study the following situations and decide how each should be handled. Write down the essential message you want to get across, and then elaborate as you role-play the situation. Provide your own specific details where necessary. Try role-playing the situation in front of the group so that everyone will get a chance to observe, comment, and make suggestions for improvement.

1. You are scheduled to work on a Saturday. Make a request, asking one of your co-workers to switch shifts with you. Give a reason as to why you can't work.

2. One of your co-workers has asked if you could work for him on Saturday. You really don't want to. Apologize and make an excuse.

3. You are supposed to be at work at 8:00 A.M., but at 7:30 there is a family emergency. Call the office and state the problem. Give reasons.

4. One of your co-workers explains to you that she has more work than she feels she can possibly handle. Make a suggestion.

5. Your boss confronts you with the fact that you have been taking long lunch hours. Respond to his criticism; admit fault and make a promise.

6. As you get to your car in the morning to drive to work, you realize that your car has a flat tire. Call into work, ask to talk to your boss, and explain the problem. Apologize and explain what you are planning to do about getting to work. Tell your boss when he can expect you at work.

7. A co-worker keeps going up to your desk and borrowing supplies, such as scissors, pens, and rulers. You don't mind sharing, but this co-worker never returns things and you are tired of having to ask him what he did with these items. Express your dissatisfaction.

8. You were supposed to meet an important business associate downtown for lunch at noon. Somehow the meeting completely slipped your mind until a co-worker mentioned it. It is five minutes until noon. It will take

you at least twenty minutes to drive downtown. Discuss the best way to handle the situation with your partner and then role-play the situation.

9. A co-worker comes to work in the morning with eyes swollen from crying. When you ask her what the matter is, she explains that she has had an argument with her husband. Apparently he wants her to quit working and stay home and take care of the children. Listen to her problems, reassure her, and make a suggestion if appropriate.

10. Your best friend had a birthday and you spent most of the night at the party celebrating. The next morning you feel so exhausted that you can't possibly see how you can get out of bed, let alone go to work. Call work and explain why you won't be coming in.

chapter 3

DOMAIN:

"Is This Really My Job?"

Courtesy U.S. Census Bureau

INTRODUCTION

In this chapter what we call *domain* refers to a person's normal or appropriate sphere of influence or area of activity. When we talk about work, one's domain is his or her area of responsibility, authority, and activity. In the next chapter, which discusses register, we will see that much of our communication is influenced by the social relationships between individuals. At work, social relationships are determined by organizational hierarchies. In a hierarchy, those at the top have a greater sphere of authority than those at the bottom. However, their domain of activity is different from the domain of those at the bottom. For example, a president of a company has authority over all members of the organization, including clerks and maintenance personnel; however, a president would not think of filing papers or of sweeping the floors, because a president's activity domain is different from that of other people in the organization. Consequently, domain refers to those activities that are properly part of one's job.

One formal way of defining an employee's normal domain of duties and responsibilities is the *job description.* A job description is a written statement that explains what you are normally expected to do. Sometimes when employees are asked to do something they feel is clearly outside of their job description, they will complain or ask for clarification. For example, if you were an engineer, you might find it strange if you were asked to type some memos for your boss, because typing memos is usually the responsibility of clerical employees. If you were a female administrative assistant, you might resent being asked to serve coffee to a group of men, because serving is the job of a waiter or waitress. You might feel that you were being taken advantage of just because you were a woman.

We can think of domain as being related not only to what we do, as in the case of job duties, but also as being related to the kinds of things we normally may or may not talk about. In this sense domain is related to what is considered personal or private information as opposed to what is considered nonpersonal or open information. Ideas about what is personal and what is nonpersonal are influenced by one's native culture. In some cultures it is all right to ask an acquaintance how much he or she paid for something. In the United States we may ask someone only under certain conditions. For example, if you did not know a co-worker extremely well, it would be inappropriate to ask how much his or her new suit cost. This information is usually considered a part of one's personal domain. However, if you ask a co-worker if he or she knows how much a new Corvette costs (and he or she does not own one), then your question is within an impersonal domain and the question is appropriate.

At work there is another dimension of what we can normally talk about and what we may not talk about. Here the distinction not only is

between personal and nonpersonal information, but is one of *work-related* as opposed to purely *social* or nonwork-related information. At work most of the conversation is usually related to the job. However, there is also a social dimension to work that we should not overlook. In many work environments some casual conversation frequently takes place, not only during lunches and breaks but also during working hours. However, each work environment usually has a slightly different view of what amount of socializing is permissible during working hours. Some organizations may not allow any, whereas others might tolerate quite a bit as long as it does not interfere with getting the job done.

Domain is also important in terms of rules of conduct, which are established by the company or even by law. In the United States there are federal laws that have jurisdiction over some of our behavior. For example, tax laws have some jurisdiction over all individuals who earn income or own property. States also have jurisdiction over much of our behavior. States, for example, may establish their own tax laws or laws governing transportation. The only restriction on the states is that the domain of their laws cannot extend beyond their borders and cannot conflict with federal laws. Most companies and organizations also establish certain rules of behavior and conduct. Companies may establish their own rules as long as these are not in conflict with laws established by the federal government, state government, local county, local city, and so on. The rules of conduct of a company are valid as long as one is at work or is being paid by the company. If, for example, one is a traveling representative of a company and is paid to travel, then he or she must adhere to company rules even when not in company buildings.

Even within an organization, sometimes there is conflict between two authorities. In an organization that has a strong union, it is not uncommon for the union to order its workers to do one thing and for management to order them to do another. If you were a union worker and were asked to go on strike, you might feel pressure from two conflicting authorities.

Being able to recognize the appropriate domain of responsibility, authority, personal familiarity, and conduct will greatly improve your skill at communicating effectively in the real world.

VOCABULARY CHECK

Match the following terms with the numbered phrase below that best explains the term or concept.

_____ a. domain

_____ b. personal

_____ c. nonpersonal

_____ d. rules of conduct

_____ e. strike

_____ f. job description

_____ g. adhere to

_____ h. hierarchy

_____ i. socializing

_____ j. conflicting

1. open, not private
2. work stoppage because of employee discontent
3. statement of employment duties and responsibilities
4. area of influence, activity, or responsibility
5. private
6. follow or conform to
7. regulations and/or expectations regarding behavior

   8. conversing about nonwork-related matters

   9. a system of grades or levels within organizations

 10. contradictory

QUESTIONS FOR DISCUSSION

1. What is meant by domain?

2. Explain the meaning of hierarchy.

3. What is a job description?

4. What is personal information? Explain.

5. What types of things are considered personal in your culture?

6. What is meant by nonpersonal information?

7. Is communication at work only business related? Explain.

8. Explain the meaning of jurisdiction.

9. What is meant by conflicting authorities?

10. Can you think of an example of conflicting authorities besides union/ employer conflicts?

DOMAIN AND HIERARCHIES

Job Descriptions: _Formal Domains_

Job descriptions are formal written descriptions or summaries of what employees are required to do while on the job. Study the following job descriptions of employees in a fictional company. Pay particular attention to each employee's duties. Are the duties specific or general? To whom does each employee report? Which employees have responsibilities to oversee, supervise, evaluate, authorize work, and/or establish policies and procedures? As you look at each job description, also try to determine with whom each employee has contact on a regular basis.

Custodian:

Responsible for routine cleaning of the interior facilities of the company. Routinely sweeps, waxes, vacuums, and dusts offices. Reports to the Building Maintenance Supervisor.

Courtesy of AT&T

Maintenance Engineer:

Responsible for routinely inspecting and repairing company facilities. Replaces and fixes faulty equipment. Repairs windows and fixtures. Inspects overall maintenance condition of facilities and prepares work orders. Reports to the Building Maintenance Supervisor.

Building Maintenance Supervisor:

Supervises and makes daily work assignments for custodial and maintenance staff. Assesses overall facilities' cleaning and condition. Authorizes minor work orders. Evaluates custodial and maintenance staff assignments. Reports to the Operations Manager.

Clerk Typist:

Primary responsibilities include providing clerical support to the division of Administrative Services. Types office correspondence, data reports, memoranda; files, answers incoming calls, and takes messages for the division. Reports to the Clerical Supervisor.

Clerical Supervisor:

Supervises clerical team. Assigns daily work schedules for clerical staff. Checks routine work for accuracy. Coordinates data, reports, and typing work load with the Data Supervisor. Makes oral and written progress reports to the Data Manager.

Data Analyst:

Analyzes production costs, output capabilities, and production performance. Projects future costs, needs, and capabilities. Submits written analysis to the Data Supervisor. Reports to the Data Supervisor.

Data Supervisor:

Supervises data team. Assigns and supervises daily work schedules for data analysts. Evaluates clerical staff assignments. Reports to Data Manager.

Administrative Assistant:

Provides general administrative support to the Data Manager. Acts as a liaison to other departments. Assists in policy formulation. Reports to the Data Manager.

Data Manager:

Oversees all office functions. Manages office staff. Reviews and evaluates Clerical Supervisor, Data Supervisor, and Administrative Assistant. Allocates and schedules major project assignments. Establishes office policies. Conducts office meetings. Determines training needs of staff. Reports to the Vice-President of Administration and Operations.

Operations Manager:

Oversees all facilities operations. Authorizes major repairs and building work orders. Authorizes all equipment orders. Evaluates Building Maintenance Supervisor. Reports to the Vice-President of Administration and Operations.

Administrative Services Secretary:

Provides administrative secretarial support to the Vice-President of Administration and Operations. Prepares correspondence, reports, and memoranda for the Vice-President. Screens incoming calls. Schedules meetings and appointments for the Vice-President. Records and transcribes transactions of administrative meetings. Reports directly to the Vice-President.

Vice-President of Administration and Operations:

Oversees the departments of Data Management and Facilities Operations. Ensures that department policies, goals, and procedures conform to general company policies, goals, and procedures, Reviews and evaluates the performance and needs of the departments of Data Management and Facilities Operations. Formulates annual goals. Reviews and evaluates the performance of the Data Manager, the Operations Manager, and the Administrative Secretary. Reports to the Company President.

PROBLEMS FOR ANALYSIS AND DISCUSSION

On the basis of the job descriptions above, answer the following questions.

1. If the Data Analyst had a problem related to data, to whom should he or she go for clarification? Explain.
2. If you were the Data Manager, and if your window were broken, whom would you call to fix it? Explain.
3. If you were the Vice-President of Administration and Operations, and if you wanted a status report on the condition of the facilities, whom would you contact? Explain.
4. If you were the Clerical Supervisor and your office had not been properly cleaned, whom would you contact? Explain.
5. If you were the Data Analyst and you needed something typed, to whom would you make your request? Explain.

CASE FOR ANALYSIS AND DISCUSSION

Job descriptions, in addition to being formal descriptions of the domain of one's work activity and responsibility, are also descriptions of formal authority in formal hierarchy. On the basis of the job descriptions just presented, match the job title with the appropriate box on the organizational chart that follows. Note that subordinate positions are on the bottom.

ORGANIZATIONAL CHART

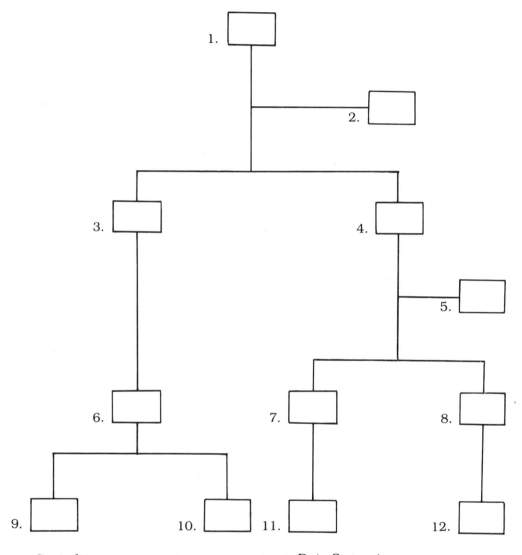

a. Custodian
b. Clerical Supervisor
c. Data Analyst
d. Maintenance Engineer
e. Operations Manager
f. Building Maintenance
   Supervisor

g. Data Supervisor
h. Administrative Assistant
j. Data Manager
k. Administrative Services Secretary
l. Vice President of Administration
   and Operations
m. Clerk Typist

COMPANY BUSINESS VERSUS
PERSONAL BUSINESS

Imagine a small company in which a young man is working as a salesman. The young man decides to use the company telephone to call his girlfriend and discuss plans for dinner. His supervisor overhears the discussion and admonishes him to make personal calls "on his own time!" (rather than on company time).

In the United States it is common for individuals to make a strong distinction between *personal time* and *company time*. In the past it was not unusual for some organizations to try to regulate their employees away from work. Schoolteachers, for example, had to be models of moral conduct not only in the class but also in their social life. Some companies even today are concerned about how well their employees represent the company both at work and at play. On the whole, however, one's free time is usually seen as one's own private business.

Mark Mangold/U.S. Census Bureau

PROBLEMS FOR ANALYSIS AND DISCUSSION

Analyze the following cases and decide whether the behavior is appropriate or inappropriate in the situation. Explain your answer in the space provided.

Case 1

Mostafa has been invited to go to lunch with his boss. At lunch, his boss says that because he is familiar with the menu, he will order for both of them. His boss orders two bacon, lettuce, and tomato sandwiches. Mostafa is embarrassed because it is against his religion to eat pork. Consequently, he politely tells his boss that he would prefer to eat something else because his religion forbids him to eat pork. Was Mostafa's behavior appropriate or inappropriate? Explain.

Case 2

Ter Phong is an assistant manager for a small company. He is normally allowed two weeks of vacation per year. In addition, he is allowed sick leave and one day of personal leave per month. Ter has already taken his vacation time. Outside of work, Ter plays soccer for a local cultural association to which he belongs. The association is having a championship series and wants Ter to play. The series will take two weeks. Ter requested two additional weeks off but was denied leave by his supervisor. Do you think that decision was fair? Explain.

Case 3

Fredrico works for a large manufacturing firm. In order to meet the demand for additional production during the Christmas rush, his company has a policy that states no personal leave will be granted between September and December. Fredrico's father passed away on September 23. Fredrico has requested a leave to go out of state to the funeral and be with the family. Fredrico's supervisor reminds him of the policy and refuses to approve the request. Do you feel the supervisor's action is appropriate? Explain.

Another type of problem arises when personal problems begin to affect performance at work. Analyze the following case and briefly explain your answer.

Case 4

Marge is going through a divorce with her husband. Marge wants to talk to someone to explain her problems. At first, Marge begins to explain her problem to you during break time. Later Marge begins to interrupt your work to explain her problems. How will you handle the situation? Explain.

DOMAINS OF CONDUCT

Conduct on the job is generally evaluated in terms of one's performance and one's attendance. In addition, most large organizations have written rules that apply to dishonesty and other types of misconduct.

Ken Karp

PROBLEMS FOR ANALYSIS AND DISCUSSION

Study the following list. Which of the following acts of misconduct do you feel to be the most serious? Rate each act of misconduct as either (S) serious, or (M) minor. Discuss your answers and your reasons with the class after everyone has finished.

_____ 1. selling drugs to fellow employees while at work

_____ 2. gambling on the job

_____ 3. being ten minutes late five times in one month

_____ 4. using drugs on the job

_____ 5. lying about an important matter to your supervisor

_____ 6. calling in sick to get extra vacation time

_____ 7. wasting time at work on a regular basis

_____ 8. drinking alcohol while working

_____ 9. using a company car for personal business

_____ 10. using the company phone for personal calls

_____ 11. having several drinks during lunch

_____ 12. borrowing a company typewriter without asking permission but returning it the next day

_____ 13. punching in a time card for a friend who will be a little late

_____ 14. taking 30 minutes on a 15-minute break

_____ 15. working on your personal bills rather than on assigned work

ANALYZING YOUR ANSWERS
FOR RULES OF CONDUCT

Depending on the organization, all of the above could be serious acts of misconduct, but let's review them case by case.

Question 1

Obviously, this would not only be serious, it would be illegal and could result not only in dismissal but possibly in legal action as well.

Question 2

Gambling would be considered a serious offense in most organizations and would also be illegal in most localities. However, a minor form of betting is common in many companies. Office pools are sometimes organized just prior to a major sports event such as the World Series or the Superbowl. In a pool, small bets of one or two dollars are placed on the score or outcome of a big game. Money is collected from co-workers. Pools are done informally rather than as part of company policy. In fact, since pools are a minor form of gambling, they may be considered violations of strict company rules, but in the case of "big games" the rules are sometimes overlooked. If you work in a place where pools are sometimes formed, we recommend that you not be the one to organize them.

Question 3

Being a few minutes late five times in a month could be considered serious by some companies where rules are strictly enforced. In other organizations a boss might not even say anything about it, but in most cases supervisors and co-workers would notice it.

Question 4

Same as question 1

Question 5

Lying, especially about something important, would normally be seen as very serious and could result in dismissal.

Question 6

Some employees occasionally use their sick time as vacation time. To discourage this practice, companies sometimes require employees to bring in notes from their doctors. If one always seems to be getting sick around holidays and vacations, supervisors will probably take notice.

Question 7

In most jobs there are occasional lulls (slow periods); however, even during slowdowns wasting time on a regular basis could be seen as serious. During normal or busy times it would be seen as very serious by most supervisors and resented by most co-workers.

Question 8

Drinking at work would be seen as very serious in most cases. However, social drinking (one or two drinks) during business lunches outside the office is common. Also during Christmas and New Year's some companies allow alcohol in company parties. We recommend that you not be the one to bring alcohol unless you are absolutely certain that you have company approval (and if you do drink, have someone who doesn't drink drive you home).

Question 9

In most cases using a company car for personal business would be seen as a serious matter. However, in some well-paying jobs the company may provide some employees with cars for both company and personal use.

Question 10

If there is an important reason to use the company phone (as in an emergency), most supervisors would allow you to do so; however, most companies have policies restricting telephone use at least for nonmanagement positions. In some jobs you may have your own phone and possibly even unrestricted use of it even for long-distance calls, but remember that most supervisors would frown upon (informally not approve of) abusing the business purpose for having the phone.

Question 11

Many people have "a" drink during lunch. Having several on a regular basis might be noticed by others and might also interfere with your work.

Question 12

Although an employee might feel tempted to borrow equipment for personal use, if equipment were borrowed without going through proper channels, it could be seen as serious. In fact, if permission were not received first, borrowing could be perceived as stealing.

Question 13

It is possible that a co-worker might ask you to punch him in (punch his time card for him). Although the request might seem harmless at the time, many organizations would view this as very serious and may even have a policy that requires both employees involved to be dismissed.

Question 14

Taking a few minutes extra on a break or a lunch is easy to do. Whether this would be seen as serious or minor again depends upon the organization. Remember, even if you work for a company that is lax (weak about enforcing the rules), others will notice those who frequently take long breaks.

Question 15

To bring in your personal bills or personal work may occasionally seem tempting, but most organizations would not tolerate your doing your personal work on company time.

DOMAINS OF AUTHORITY

Employee/employer relationships are not equal, since employers hold the dominant position; however, there are restrictions on the authority of employers over employees. Foremost of these is the restriction against discrimination. As we mentioned at the beginning of this chapter, laws of the federal government have jurisdiction over all other laws and rules. According to the 1964 Civil Rights Act, discrimination on the basis of sex, race, religion, or national origin is illegal. For this reason, women and minorities cannot be excluded from any job. For example, a police department cannot exclude women from being policewomen just because it feels that the job is too dangerous.

Companies can, however, require that all employees adhere to a particular dress code or grooming code. A company may, for example, require all men to wear suits and all women to wear pant suits or dresses. If a com-

Courtesy of IBM

pany establishes a dress code, the code must apply both to men and women but would not have to require both of them to dress in exactly the same way. However, it would be illegal for a company to establish a dress code only for women.

PROBLEMS FOR ANALYSIS AND DISCUSSION

Study the following cases and try to determine whether the action taken was proper or improper. Briefly explain your reasons in the space provided.

Pregnancy

Case 1

Nadia has just informed her boss that, because she is pregnant, she will be taking four months' leave of absence in about two months. Her boss says he will not allow her to take a leave for that reason and that she will have to quit. Do you feel her boss is acting properly? Explain.

Case 2

Mari is pregnant. She wants to take off six months from work and then return to her job. While she is off, she wants to collect disability insurance to help pay for her expenses. Do you feel that Mari should be allowed to collect the insurance? Explain.

Religion

Case 1

Alice is Catholic and Rosslin is Jewish. Both work at a large department store that is open seven days per week. Both work in the Personnel Department. Both get two days off per week, but they do not get the same two days off because at least one must be in the office every day to handle the normal responsibilities of the office. Both are also very religious. Alice goes to church every Sunday, and Rosslin goes to the synagogue every Saturday. A new store rule states that all employees must work on Saturday. Do you feel that Rosslin should also work on Saturday if the job can be covered by Alice? Explain.

Case 2

Alaa works for a large international company. The company is having its annual Christmas party. Alaa is a member of a non-Christian religion. Alaa feels uncomfortable about participating in the party. He has decided not to attend. Is his behavior within his rights? Explain.

Employee Dress Codes

Case 1

Salesco is a small sales office that employs about twenty salesmen and about ten saleswomen. The office manager just put out a memo stating that all the women must wear dresses of a particular style. No mention was made regarding dress codes for men. Was this proper? Explain.

Hiring Practices

Case 1

An airline company has just advertised stewardess positions for women ages 18–33. Do you feel that this is proper? Explain.

Case 2

A packing company has stated that all applicants who wish to apply for a position loading boxes into trucks must be able to lift 40 pounds at least 5 feet off the ground. Should the company give such a test? Explain.

FROM THEORY TO PRACTICE: TRYING IT ON YOUR OWN

In order to try out what you have learned, practice the following role-playing situations either in small groups or in front of the class. Those observ-

Laimute E. Druskis/Taurus Photos

ing should comment on how effectively those in the role-playing exercise perform. Observers should make notes in the space provided.

Situation 1

Marsha works for an electronics company. She is requesting medical leave for four months because she is going to have a baby. The company is currently in a rush period. Normally, if someone leaves during such a period, he or she must be replaced. No personal leaves are being given at this time. Remember: Marsha is requesting a medical leave. As you consider this situation, it is important to remember both what the law is and what the needs of the company are.

PERSON A:

Assume that you are Marsha's supervisor. Marsha will approach you with her request for medical leave. Remember what the company's needs are.

PERSON B:

Assume that you are Marsha. Make your request for medical leave, and remember what your rights are.

OBSERVER NOTES:

Situation 2

Danilo is an employee in a manufacturing company. Company policy allows for each employee to have three weeks' vacation time per year. Danilo's family lives overseas. He has been invited to go home to attend his brother's wedding. In addition, his father has suggested that he take some extra time off from work and stay with the family for a total of about six weeks. In this situation it is important for us to look at the request from Danilo's point of view and to consider it from the company's point of view.

Rhoda Sidney/Monkmeyer Press

PERSON A:

You are Danilo's supervisor. It is important for you to represent company policy properly, but it is also important that you be sensitive to the special problems of employees. You must also carefully consider how other employees will view your decisions.

PERSON B:

You are Danilo. You want to keep your job, but you would also really appreciate being able to get six weeks off, because you have not visited your family for several years. You must be careful in how you make your request. If you push too hard, it might cause a serious conflict between you and your supervisor.

OBSERVER NOTES:

Situation 3

An office supervisor has been told by the department manager that too many employees have been making personal calls on department phones. This is a violation of company policy. The department manager has asked the office supervisor to watch for violators of the policy. The supervisor is to remind them about the policy and to warn them not to violate it again. During the day, the supervisor notices two individuals using the phones for personal use and speaks to each person privately (first to person B and later to person C). It is important that the supervisor be firm but sensitive. It is also important that the employees explain why they have used the phone if there was any special or unusual need to do so.

PERSON A:

You are the office supervisor. First make sure that each employee knows what the company policy is regarding the personal use of the phones. Next try to find out why the person used the phone. Be firm but also reasonable and sensitive.

PERSON B:

You are an office worker who has just used the phone to call a friend about some dinner arrangements you have made for next week. As you listen to the supervisor, consider whether the use of the phone was necessary or urgent, and be open to your supervisor's point of view.

PERSON C:

You are an office worker who has just used the office phone to make a call to your child's school. You called because you found a note on your desk saying that the school nurse was trying to contact you about your child. Consider the importance of your call, and also consider your supervisor's position and point of view. Be certain to explain your special circumstance.

OBSERVER NOTES:

Situation 4

Elina works at a large insurance company. In addition to her job, she has recently started selling cosmetics to earn some extra income. Elina has been showing samples to other employees during her lunch hour. Recently Elina has also started trying to take orders during her break. During her break she has been going into various offices where other employees are working, who are not on break, and trying to interest them in taking orders. Several other supervisors have complained to Elina's supervisor about Elina's interrupting their employees' work.

The important thing to remember in this situation is the difference between personal time and company time.

PERSON A:

You are Elina's supervisor. Elina's behavior at work reflects not only on her but also on you, since you are responsible for supervising her work. Talk to Elina about the problem. Try to get her to see how others in the company view what she is doing. Decide whether you will ask her to stop taking orders completely, or whether some compromise is possible.

PERSON B:

You are Elina. You feel you are a hard-working employee. You take orders only during lunch time and break time. You need the extra money to supplement your income. When you take orders on your break, you try not to interrupt the work of others for more than a minute or two. Be sensitive to your supervisor's view of the problem.

OBSERVER NOTES:

chapter **4**

REGISTER USE:

"How Should You Say It?"

AFL-CIO News

INTRODUCTION

As you have seen from studying the various language functions, communication is a complex process. It involves sending and receiving messages from people at all levels of the organization; consequently, chances for misunderstandings are great. At times, an employee may be intending to send one message but may end up communicating something completely different. For example, a worker whose intention is to tell his boss about a problem and ask for time off may say: "You have to give me the afternoon off. I have a dentist appointment." The message the supervisor receives will be that the employee is giving orders and assuming an authority that he does not have. The boss, who under normal circumstances does not mind excusing his employees for medical appointments, may react negatively and insist that the particular worker spend the time on the job and reschedule the appointment after work hours or Saturdays. His message may be: "I don't have to do anything you tell me. After all, I am the boss around here." The employee, in turn, may not understand why he is being treated differently from the rest of the people on the job and may interpret the boss's message as: "The boss doesn't like me. He goes out of his way to give me a hard time." This interpretation is probably invalid. In fact, the boss is simply trying to assert his authority over his subordinate and show him who is in charge. It is easy to see how inappropriate language of this type can affect relationships at work.

In order to make the correct decision on what communication to use with people at work, you will need to know where you stand in that organization. That is, you need to know where you stand in the company and what role you are expected to play. The methods you use for interacting and the language you choose to communicate will need to change according to the position of the people you are dealing with. Most of your time at work will probably be spent communicating with your co-workers, but often you will have to talk to your supervisor as well. If you are in any kind of supervisory position yourself, you will also need to know how to handle the people who report to you.

Most of us have learned to vary our language and our behavior to meet the needs of different circumstances. We may feel free to yell and shout at children when we are angry with them, but we are usually very careful about raising our voices to our bosses or to other authority figures. We may tease our friends or joke around with them, but we tend to be more serious with strangers. We may accept hugs and kisses from other members of our family, but many of us get uncomfortable when people we don't know very well touch us. Besides these obvious signals by which we communicate familiarity, there are more subtle messages that we send to show whether other people are close friends or whether the relationship is more distant. These subtle changes may include slight differences in language ("may I talk to you" versus "can I talk to you"), eye contact (longer with friends than with strangers), and other forms of nonverbal behavior. In general, closeness and distance and subsequent register use between employees are determined by the company hierarchy: many employees get along well with the people who have the same responsibilities as they do and thus use the kind of language with them that they would use with their friends; however, since the relationship with superiors tends to be rather distant, the language used with bosses tends to be much more formal. This change becomes particularly evident in cases where a former buddy is promoted and friends suddenly find themselves in a superior/subordinate relationship. Here quite often problems arise and the friendship ends, as a result of the fact that language and behavior that are common between friends (such as asking for and giving advice, asking and granting personal favors) are usually inappropriate to use in superior/subordinate relationships. Even though there are no hard and fast rules that govern register use between people at work, there are a number of unwritten rules that employees can follow.

Adjusting your language, your style, and your communication strategies according to your position and that of others in the company is called *register use*. In order to handle register use properly, you will need to understand how positions in a company are organized and how information flows within an organization. This chapter will give you an understanding of company structures and organizational information flow and will show you how to adapt your language for effective register use.

VOCABULARY CHECK

Match each of the following terms with the numbered phrase that best explains the concept. Note that two of the numbered phrases do not match any of the terms.

_____ a. register use

_____ b. authority

_____ c. familiar (familiarity)

_____ d. subtle

_____ e. subsequent

_____ f. buddy (colloquial)

1. changing your language according to the relative status of the speakers involved
2. a very good friend
3. following as a consequence; happening as a result

4. the power or responsibility to control and command
5. not obvious, barely noticeable
6. well-known
7. comfortable
8. open with

QUESTIONS FOR DISCUSSION

1. What is an employee communicating when he tells his boss, "You have to give me the afternoon off"?

2. What message was the boss sending his employee when he told him that he couldn't get time off and had to change his dentist appointment?

3. What might have been a better way to ask for time off because of a dentist appointment?

4. What do we mean by register use?

RULES FOR APPROPRIATE REGISTER USE

Subordinate to Superior

In all organizations there are unspoken rules that are followed in talking to people who have greater or lesser status than oneself. These include rules for language and tone as well as for nonverbal behavior. For example, command forms such as, "Gimme my time sheet!" or "Tell the secretary to order me some pencils" are inappropriate to use with superiors. This is also true of command forms followed by "please." For example, "Give me the day off, please" remains a command even if it is slightly softened. In order to be considered a request, it would have to be presented in a more polite form, such as: "Could I have the day off on Friday? My uncle died and I would like to go to the funeral."

As far as tone is concerned, subordinates need to find a reasonable middle ground between sounding too deferential and sounding rude. For instance, the words "I'm sorry" can be said in such a way that we imagine a humble servant begging for his master's forgiveness, or it can be said in a manner that indicates the employee considers the boss at fault and is challenging him. Consider the case of the employee who responded to his supervisor's reprimand by saying: "You never like anything I do, do you?

Well, I'm sorry. But I'm not perfect like you are." We can be quite sure that his boss did not consider that statement an apology.

Remarks such as these, in which the tone conveys a meaning that is directly opposite of what the words seem to indicate, are called _sarcastic_ remarks. Sarcasm is often used between co-workers to show dissatisfaction. For example: "The boss told me I couldn't take my vacation next month. That's just great. I really like the way they take care of their employees around here." Sometimes sarcasm is used in teasing good friends, as when one secretary sees another drink a milkshake and eat a box of cookies for lunch and asks her: "How's your diet going?" So while friendly sarcasm is often used between employees who know each other well, it really has no place in more formal relationships. Neither does it have a place when the two employees are in the company of others in a more formal situation.

Regarding nonverbal behavior, we find that as a general rule, subordinates are expected to demonstrate the same kind of respect they would show verbally. For example, employees are expected to rise from their chairs when they are being introduced to a superior and wait for the person with higher status to offer to shake hands. In many companies subordinates also hold doors open for superiors or allow them to enter or exit elevators first. However, this kind of polite behavior can create a great deal of

American Airlines

awkwardness (as when an employee has to rush by his or her boss to be the first at a door or when a group of people miss the elevator because the department manager did not step forward fast enough). Thus, many firms have adopted informal rules of etiquette dictated by common sense.

Peer to Peer

Those unspoken rules of behavior are not limited to interactions with superiors; they affect peer relationships as well. Employees who are on the same level are expected to treat each other differently than they treat their superiors. For example, a technician in the department who insists on addressing the other technicians in the department as "sir" or "ma'am" will *not* be regarded as nice and respectful but will likely be considered as "weird." Similarly, an employee who always maintains a certain distance from the rest of the group, even when personal matters are discussed, might be considered aloof and unfriendly rather than polite. In most companies employees are expected to take an interest in each other's lives and share some of their personal experiences. People who feel that their private lives are nobody's business but their own (and refuse to talk about themselves) often make themselves outsiders. Usually they are treated by the rest of the group accordingly. In addition, since valuable business information often travels through informal channels, employees who refuse to get involved with their fellow workers often shut themselves off from information that could be useful to their careers.

Irene Springer

Superior to Subordinate

In superior/subordinate relationships the rules may be even more subtle. A supervisor may use request forms ("would you . . ."; "could you . . .") when she gives work assignments even though she also has the authority to use command forms ("do this immediately"). Of course, a supervisor who chooses to speak _only_ in command forms may create resentment and hostility among the work force, while a superior who treats her subordinates politely and shows respect for their feelings often gets greater cooperation from her staff. Ideally a superior would mix decisiveness and strength with sensitivity and consideration. As a general rule, we may say that the lower the level of the work, the more command forms and orders seem to appear in the language used by supervisors. The higher the level of the employee and the more professional the work being done, the more often we find requests and other forms of polite language being used by superiors.

Regarding nonverbal behavior, it may be acceptable for a superior to lightly touch a subordinate on the back or on the arm, especially when expressing sympathy or encouragement, but conversely, a subordinate generally does not have that option. While many employees don't object to friendly pats on the back, there are a number of people who find being touched by a superior patronizing. Touching and being touched have become such sensitive areas that a safe strategy for supervisory personnel may be, "When in doubt, don't touch."

VOCABULARY CHECK

Match each of the following terms with the numbered phrase below that best explains the concept. Two of the numbered phrases do not match any of the terms.

_____ a. deferential

_____ b. status

_____ c. sarcastic remarks

_____ d. out of line (colloquial)

_____ e. weird

_____ f. aloof

_____ g. resentment

_____ h. hostility

_____ i. condescending

_____ j. patronize

_____ k. prerogative

1. very humble, showing exaggerated respect
2. breaking social rules; not showing proper respect
3. not obvious, barely noticeable
4. words spoken in a joking manner with the tone indicating that the opposite message is intended, such as saying, "Great day, isn't it?" when the weather is particularly bad
5. position, prestige
6. the power or right to control and command
7. a feeling of bitterness or anger because the other person is unfair or is taking advantage of the situation
8. treat someone that you are helping in a way that makes him or her feel inferior
9. acting nicely, but at the same time showing that you are superior
10. special right or privilege
11. distant, unfriendly, not willing to take part in something
12. anger, hatred, ill will
13. strange, odd

QUESTIONS FOR DISCUSSION

1. What is meant by superior-to-subordinate communication?
2. What does it mean to sound deferential?
3. What are sarcastic remarks?
4. Is it ever acceptable to be sarcastic at work? Explain.
5. Give some examples of appropriate and inappropriate nonverbal behavior.
6. What is meant by peer-to-peer behavior?
7. Give some examples of weird or aloof peer-to-peer behavior.
8. What is superior-to-subordinate behavior?
9. Does a superior have a right to use command forms? Explain.
10. Is it appropriate that a supervisor always use command forms?

PROBLEMS FOR ANALYSIS AND DISCUSSION

Test yourself to see to what degree you understand the rules of register use in the workplace. Look at the numbered responses that follow and decide in each case whether the language or the behavior would be acceptable to use in any of the relationships outlined. In some cases the response does not fit any relationship and must be considered inappropriate. Choose one of the following for each answer.

    a. peer-to-peer relationship

    b. subordinate-to-superior relationship

    c. superior-to-subordinate relationship

    d. inappropriate

You may wish to discuss the problems in pairs or small groups so that you can compare your answers. In some cases, more than one answer is possible.

    1. "We seem to be having a problem. I would like to see you in my office in about fifteen minutes."

    2. "We seem to be having a problem. Maybe we'd better get together after lunch and talk about it. What do you think?"

    3. "Please, sir, you must hire my friend; he will be the best worker you've ever had."

    4. "If you don't hire my friend, you are making a big mistake."

    5. "I am sure you are aware that personal phone calls are unacceptable."

    6. "You'd better watch out. If they catch you making personal phone calls, you'll be in trouble."

    7. "Would you loan me five dollars for lunch? I am a little short on cash right now."

    8. "I wonder if you can be so kind as to loan me five dollars. I seem to be somewhat short of cash."

    9. "How was you vacation? Did you meet any interesting women?"

    10. "Did you enjoy your vacation?"

    11. "I want these letters out by tomorrow morning. Every single one of them. And don't tell me that it can't be done."

    12. "How am I supposed to finish these letters by tomorrow? What am I, a robot or something?"

    13. "You are an extremely attractive young woman, Miss Jones, and I am sure you will go far in this organization. I will expect

you to come to my apartment this evening so that we can discuss your future with this company."

_____ 14. "There will be a convention in Houston next month, Ms. Kurata, and I expect you to come along as my assistant."

_____ 15. "Mr. Brown, the supervisor , is always ridiculing me and making me feel stupid. He is making me miserable. I don't know what to do."

_____ 16. "I'm upset because you seem to be unhappy with the work I'm doing. Could you explain to me in detail what I am doing wrong?"

_____ 17. "I want you to repeat that. I don't understand what you are saying."

_____ 18. "I'm having real trouble figuring out what you are saying. Could you slow down a little?"

CHAIN OF COMMAND

As you saw in the chapter on domain, most companies have an organization that is hierarchical; that is, they have a structure in which power flows

AT&T Co. Photo Center

from the top through successive layers to the bottom. The person who occupies the top position has more authority than anyone else, and the people at the bottom have the least to say as to what decisions should be made. The hierarchical structure resembles a pyramid, with the president of the company on the top, members of midlevel management across the center, and hourly wage earners at the lowest level.

As a general rule, the president of the company is the only person who does not have to report to anyone else (though he or she may report to a board of directors). Those at the bottom of the hierarchy, on the other hand, only follow instructions; they do not assign work to anyone else. At all other levels, an employee is both a superior, or someone who is responsible for other people's work, and a subordinate, or someone who is responsible to someone else and receives instructions from above. Power, status, and responsibility decrease as we move down the pyramid. Since people on top are seen as having greater authority than people at midlevels, and since their work is considered of greater importance, they receive higher pay and greater respect for their work. This respect is paid not necessarily because the person is a better human being or works harder than other employees; rather it is awarded because of the position the employee holds within the company hierarchy.

Theoretically, hierarchies are set up in such a way that each employee reports to one person only. The employee is responsible to one boss and receives instructions and directives from him or her only. The structure is set up this way to avoid situations in which different superiors give conflicting instructions to the same subordinate.

In an organization that has a hierarchical structure, employees generally receive their instructions from their immediate supervisors. Those supervisors in turn report to *their* bosses, who are responsible to the superiors directly above *them*. This structure is referred to as the *chain of command* (see chapter 3). When reporting information, asking for clarification, making requests, delivering complaints, or performing other communicative functions, employees are expected to follow the established order of authority. Employees who go over their supervisor's head and thus disregard the chain of command are often regarded as troublemakers and are treated accordingly.

PROBLEM FOR ANALYSIS AND DISCUSSION

The following case shows that it is sometimes difficult to decide how information should flow. Examine the case and try to determine the best course of action. Compare your answers with those of the rest of the class and be prepared to defend your choice.

Case 1

Mr. Sirag is a department manager for a large computer firm. One day he gets an exciting job offer from a competing firm that is too attractive to turn down. Mr. Sirag decides to accept the job offer. He wants to let his superiors know about the move one month ahead of time to make sure they will have sufficient time to hire and train a replacement. Whom should Mr. Sirag talk to first about his upcoming job change? Choose the answer below that you think is best, and be prepared to explain your reasons.

_____ 1. Mr. Sirag should not tell anyone about his move. If he does, management will get upset and think that he is ungrateful.

_____ 2. Mr. Sirag should tell the people who work for him first. His subordinates need to get used to the idea that someone else will be their boss, and they will need time to say goodbye to him.

_____ 3. Mr. Sirag should tell his friends and co-workers first. They will be able to give him advice on whether he is making the right decision and might be able to keep him from making a mistake.

_____ 4. Mr. Sirag should tell his immediate boss first. He has the right to know what is happening in the department so that plans for the future can be made.

_____ 5. Mr. Sirag should write a letter to the president of the company first. The president is in charge of everyone and needs to know immediately when any changes will occur in his company.

_____ 6. Mr. Sirag should send his resignation to the Personnel Department first. They are in charge of handling all matters related to hiring and firing, and they will inform all the people who need to know about his move.

_____ 7. Other. Explain how you would handle the situation differently.

INFORMATION FLOW

You have seen that a company structure is set up in such a way that power travels in one direction only, from top to bottom. This is not the case for the way in which information flows. Information travels in several directions at once: Supervisors communicate with their subordinates, and subordinates in turn give feedback to their supervisors. In addition, employees talk to each other in order to facilitate social contact and solve work-related problems. Information thus mainly flows in two directions: downward and upward.

Downward Communication

Downward communication is used by superiors who want to communicate with their subordinates. The message sent may be written, oral, or nonverbal and may fulfill a variety of functions. Among these would be:

1. Delivering instructions and giving job assignments; these assignments may include when, where, how, and by whom something is to be done.

2. Providing general information about the company such as pay schedules, employee benefits, and available vacation time.

3. Evaluating job performances, both of individual employees and groups of employees working together.

4. Persuading and motivating, such as providing positive information about the organization, offering special nonmonetary incentives to workers (such as employee of the month awards), and advertising company events.

How effective downward communication is depends on how well employees understand the messages that their superiors are sending and to what degree they are willing and able to act on these messages.

Problems occur when managers send messages that are unclear or too complicated to be understood. In addition, downward communication may be ineffective if supervisors do not provide enough reasons as to why the work should be performed in a certain way. Miscommunication or lack of understanding may also result from the fact that downward communication often travels through several layers of management and may become distorted in the process.

Upward Communication

Upward communication occurs when subordinates send messages to their superiors. These messages may be sent in response to a request by management, or they may be sent spontaneously. These messages may also be oral, written, or nonverbal and may include the following functions:

1. Providing responses to information requested and giving feedback on how well (or not so well) work is progressing.

2. Giving reasons as to why certain jobs cannot or have not been done and explanations of problems that inhibit work performance.

3. Suggesting improvements and making recommendations as to how jobs can be done more efficiently or how working conditions can be improved.

4. Making requests and asking for permission such as asking for a raise, requesting more responsibility, or asking for time off.

5. Explaining personal reactions to the job, including criticism of co-workers or unhappiness with the amount of work or type of assignments given; explaining problems.

There are a number of reasons why upward communication is often not as effective as it could be. Employees sometimes don't know how to explain a problem clearly to management and often provide explanations that have nothing to do with the problems at hand. At other times upward communication may miss its mark because the employee uses inappropriate language or the wrong tone or does not have a good sense of timing.

PROBLEMS FOR ANALYSIS AND DISCUSSION

Study the following case and determine whether upward communication was used correctly. Remember that as a general rule, work-related problems should be discussed with the immediate supervisor. Compare your answers with those of the rest of the class.

Case 1

Laura is a young secretary who likes being treated as a professional employee. Unfortunately, she has an old-fashioned boss who likes to treat her as "one of the girls." He likes to ask her to make coffee for him and his guests and sometimes he asks her to buy presents for his wife. What bothers Laura most of all is that he calls her "honey" instead of using her name. Laura decides to teach him a lesson and embarrass him in front of his associates. At an important meeting, when her boss, as expected, tells her, "Listen, honey, would you mind taking notes?" she responds with righteous indignation: "Listen, sir, I am not your honey. From now on I would appreciate it very much if you could call me by my name." How do you interpret Laura's actions? Choose the answers you think best, and be prepared to explain your reasons.

_____ 1. Laura was right to object to being called honey. She was not making a "big deal out of nothing."

_____ 2. Laura was right in bringing up the topic to her boss rather than talking to someone else about it.

_____ 3. Laura was right in bringing up the topic at the meeting rather than choosing another time to discuss it.

_____ 4. Other. If you were Laura, how could you have handled the situation? What would you have said and done? Be specific.

Often employees use upward communication to express concerns about their fellow workers. They feel that their superiors should act as referees, and they expect them to manage the conflicts that arise when people with different personalities, styles, and attitudes have to work together. As a rule, superiors are concerned that everyone get along and work well together, but by the same token they often don't have the time and energy to get involved in what might be considered "personality problems."

Look at the following case and decide how the situation should be handled. Discuss your answer with your classmates.

Case 2

Mary Valdez has had a lot of problems with her co-worker Samantha Jones. Samantha is a faster worker than Mary and when she has her jobs completed, she walks over to Mary's desk to talk to her. She does not mind interrupting Mary, telling her about her personal problems and complaining about management. Mary is tired of listening to Samantha. She is especially annoyed because her co-worker's endless chatter keeps her from getting her work done. Mary would like to change the situation. What should she do? Choose the answer you think is best, and be prepared to explain your reasons.

_____ 1. Mary should tell her immediate boss about the problem. She should ask him to tell Samantha to leave her alone so that she can get her work done.

_____ 2. Mary should bypass her boss and go directly to the division manager. He has much more power than Mary's boss and will be able to get faster and longer-lasting results.

_____ 3. Mary should report the matter to the Personnel Department of her company. Personnel departments are set up to solve problems between employees and to make sure that everyone gets along.

_____ 4. Mary should ignore the situation altogether and not cause any problems. After a while, Samantha will probably get tired of talking to her and stop on her own.

_____ 5. Other. Explain how you would handle the situation.

FROM THEORY TO PRACTICE:
TRYING IT ON YOUR OWN

The following role plays are set up to give you practice in using the appropriate register in a number of practical situations. Read the situation and decide what you would say and do. Then role-play the case. (Note that cases 3, 4, and 5 need several partners.) Take turns role-playing in front of the class while observers evaluate the effectiveness of your verbal and nonverbal behavior. Use spaces below each case for observers' comments.

Case 1

You have had a chipped tooth for several days, and you have finally been able to make an appointment with your dentist for Friday morning. You assume that there will be no problem taking the time off because a number of employees have done the same in the past. On Tuesday your boss announces that there will be a staff meeting Friday morning to discuss various problems that have come up during the week. You know that if you cancel your appointment with the dentist, it might take two weeks or more until you can get another appointment. You don't want to upset your boss, but you would like to keep your appointment. Your boss understands your problem but would like to have everyone present at the meeting. How would you handle the situation?

OBSERVER NOTES:

Case 2

You are a manager in a large firm that has several secretaries who work in a "typing pool." You are applying for a job with another company and need a clean resume. You would like one of the secretaries to stay after work and type the resume for you. You know that the secretaries have been typing personal correspondence for some of the higher executives at times. You approach a secretary with your request, but she seems reluctant. What language would you use to convince her to do you that favor?

OBSERVER NOTES:

Case 3

There is a young man in your group who seems to smoke incessantly. The rest of you are bothered by the cigarette smoke and would like him to smoke outside of the building or in the employees' lounge. The young man is not very friendly and none of you wants to talk to him. Some of you think that the boss should handle the situation, while others think the problem needs to be solved by the employees themselves. Discuss the problem with the rest of the group and decide what should be done.

OBSERVER NOTES:

Case 4

You work as a clerk in a small office. Your boss is very impatient and gets nasty when you make a mistake. Two days ago she yelled at you when she found a mistake on a report you had typed. You think that the only reason you made the mistake was that your boss was making you nervous. Talk to your friends and decide whether you should talk to your boss, to her supervisor, or to the person who hired you. Then decide what you would say.

OBSERVER NOTES:

Case 5

Several days ago a co-worker handed you an important report and asked you to look it over and make comments. Today the same co-worker stops you in the hall and demands to know what happened to the report. When you explain to her that you put the report on her desk, she accuses you of lying and claims that you must have lost or misplaced it. Discuss the situation with her and report the situation to the supervisor. The supervisor listens to both of you and tries to handle the situation.

OBSERVER NOTES:

Case 6 - S-generated

chapter 5

URGENCY AND PRIORITY:
"How Important Is This?"

Courtesy of Burke Marketing Services, Inc.

INTRODUCTION

Have you ever been given an assignment that had a great deal of urgency given to it? Imagine that you were working on a routine assignment and your boss came in and said: "I've got a hot one. Get on it because I need it yesterday!" Most of us have had that experience at one time or another. However, most of the time things are not so clear-cut. Sometimes it's hard to determine which among several things is the most important or which needs the most immediate attention. Most of us tend to see things only from a short-term perspective, that is, we tend to see the importance of things that relate to the near future or that seem to have a direct relationship to our lives. Much of your success in the workplace depends upon your flexibility and ability to determine priorities. Occasionally you might be shifted to another station, and once in a great while you might encounter an emergency or crisis situation in which special action might be required.

Most of us, however, work in environments that are generally less regimented than assembly lines. Even so, our work usually follows routines

Courtesy of IBM

that are fairly predictable. Most of the time employees know what they are supposed to do. Employees who stand out over the rest, however, are usually those who understand how to be flexible, making adjustments in schedules and redefining priorities. Employees who can adapt to new priorities and quickly readjust their schedules are usually valued above those who are less adaptable.

Your understanding of how to determine urgency and importance also affects how others in the organization perceive your style. If you are able to schedule your work and meet deadlines, your supervisors will see you as being conscientious. Moreover, if you are to be seen as a valuable employee, you will need to develop the critical skills of determining urgency and importance and of setting priorities. These skills not only are important for managers and supervisors but need to be acquired by most employees.

VOCABULARY CHECK

Match each of the following terms with the numbered phrase that best explains it.

_____ a. flexibility

_____ b. urgent

_____ c. priority

_____ d. routine

_____ e. procedure

_____ f. regimented

_____ g. predictable

_____ h. emergency

_____ i. stand out

_____ j. adapt

_____ k. deadline

_____ l. conscientious

1. normal or ordinary way of doing things
2. established method or prescribed way of doing things
3. a matter of greater importance than something else
4. the ability to change or move from one thing to another thing
5. conform to a new situation

6. serious situation or crisis demanding immediate attention

7. made to conform to strict rules

8. due date

9. expected

10. alert and hard working, responsible

11. needing instant or immediate attention

12. have qualities that are more easily recognizable than others

QUESTIONS FOR DISCUSSION

1. What does urgency mean?

2. What is meant by short-term perspective?

3. What are priorities?

4. Give an example of an emergency.

5. Why is being flexible at work important?

6. What is a deadline?

SELF-ASSESSMENT_____

In the following exercise you will have the opportunity to assess your style as it relates to setting priorities, working under deadlines, and being flexible and adaptable.

For the statements that follow, try to state honestly whether or not you mostly agree or disagree. If you mostly agree, mark A. If you mostly disagree, mark D.

_____ 1. I do my best work under pressure. I prefer to wait until the last minute before starting.

_____ 2. I like to know exactly what is required of me before I do anything new. I do not like to assume responsibility unless I am absolutely sure of what I should do.

_____ 3. I like to try to figure things out alone. I do not like to ask questions unless I cannot figure something out by myself.

_____ 4. If I finish an assignment and others are still working, I usually will jump in and try to help them.

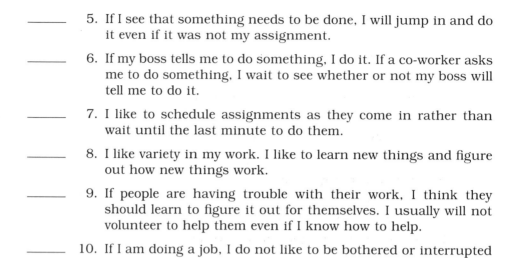

_____ 5. If I see that something needs to be done, I will jump in and do it even if it was not my assignment.

_____ 6. If my boss tells me to do something, I do it. If a co-worker asks me to do something, I wait to see whether or not my boss will tell me to do it.

_____ 7. I like to schedule assignments as they come in rather than wait until the last minute to do them.

_____ 8. I like variety in my work. I like to learn new things and figure out how new things work.

_____ 9. If people are having trouble with their work, I think they should learn to figure it out for themselves. I usually will not volunteer to help them even if I know how to help.

_____ 10. If I am doing a job, I do not like to be bothered or interrupted until I have finished.

Now compare your answers with the suggestions made in the following section.

ANALYZING YOUR ANSWERS

As we will discuss in the chapter on style and attitude, chapter 6, sometimes a weakness can be an overplayed strength. As you review your answers and read the following comments, keep that advice in mind. Remember that in most cases there are no absolutely correct or incorrect answers.

Comments on Question 1

If you do your best work under pressure, it may be that you are not establishing priorities well enough when you are not under pressure. Although being able to work well under pressure is generally an asset, if you find yourself always working under pressure, you may be getting into bad habits that could eventually lead to burnout because you fail to set priorities in advance.

Comments on Question 2

It is generally a good idea to be cautious and careful and to wait for instructions. However, most employers encourage employees to show some initiative and to think for themselves. Try to figure out minor details on your own.

Comments on Question 3

Self-reliance is generally encouraged by most employers. However, in situations where procedures and rules must be strictly followed, it is probably better to ask for clarification before doing something new. On the surface, this advice appears to contradict the advice in question 2. In reality, it depends on the attitude of your company toward rules and procedures. Try to get a feeling for the amount of initiative that your company expects people in your position to show.

Comments on Question 4

Being helpful and cooperative are usually seen as positive qualities. However, be certain that helping others does not keep you from finishing your own work.

Comments on Question 5

Again, initiative is generally a positive quality. However, be careful not to overstep your authority so that you are not criticized for being presumptuous.

Comments on Question 6

Sometimes it is a good idea to get clarification from your boss before helping others. However, in the case of small requests, it is usually all right to be cooperative. But keep in mind that your own work needs to take priority.

Comments on Question 7

Scheduling assignments as they come in (in sequence) is usually the best way to avoid burnout, unless a late assignment has a higher priority.

Comments on Question 8

Many people enjoy having some variety in their work and enjoy learning new skills. Sometimes, however, you have to work, at least temporarily, in a job that is routine and allows for little variety.

Comments on Question 9

Although it is usually better to allow others the opportunity to solve their own problems, there is generally no harm in lending a helping hand, especially if they are racing to meet a deadline. Again, be certain that you do not always get stuck helping others and end up ignoring your own work.

Comments on Question 10

Most of us need to concentrate on our work to be effective and productive, but we also need to be flexible when an interruption is unavoidable because it is a higher priority.

TOOLS TO HELP YOU ESTABLISH PRIORITIES AND SCHEDULE ACTIVITIES

There is no foolproof method for setting priorities and scheduling activities, as the following story helps to illustrate. There is an old joke in this country about a man who could never remember what he was supposed to buy when he went to the market, so his friend suggested that he tie a string around his finger to help him remember. When he got to the market, someone asked him why he had a string tied around his finger. He replied that it was to help him remember what he was supposed to buy. When he was asked what he wanted, he replied that he had forgotten!

Although no scheduling device is foolproof, there are a number of aids that can help you to manage your time and set priorities. Most of us have a

VISTA

monthly calendar at home hanging in our kitchen or study, or one in the office. The trick is to get into the habit of writing down key dates on the calendar and then checking the calendar on a regular basis. A device similar to a calendar is a _planner_. This is much like a small book that you can carry with you to write down important dates and brief notes. Again, the trick is to remember to use it and to refer to it on a regular basis.

Another useful device is a _time chart_. When you are scheduling a number of activities or a major project over a number of months, a time chart allows you to have an overview of the time relationships. Whereas a calendar or planner tends to focus on one day, week, or month at a time, a time chart allows you to see a comprehensive picture.

Study the following example of a time chart for a sales campaign.

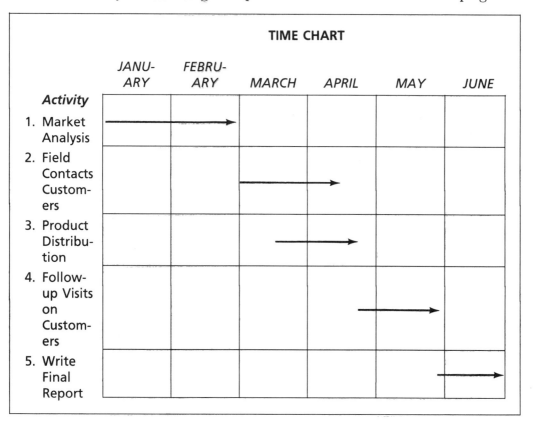

TIME CHART

Activity	JANU-ARY	FEBRU-ARY	MARCH	APRIL	MAY	JUNE
1. Market Analysis	————	———→				
2. Field Contacts Customers			————	——→		
3. Product Distribution			———	——→		
4. Follow-up Visits on Customers				————	——→	
5. Write Final Report					———	——→

PROBLEMS FOR ANALYSIS AND DISCUSSION

Imagine that you have been asked to study a major operation within your organization. At the conclusion of your study you will have to make a final report and then visit other branches outside your office and present the findings of your study.

Here is a list of the activities that you must perform and the anticipated length of time each activity will take. The order below does not represent the order in which you will actually do the activities.

Activities	Estimated Time Necessary
a. Write a final report	One month
b. Collect data	Three months
c. Present final report at other branches	One month
d. Analyze data collected	One month
e. Hold planning meetings to decide what staff will be needed	One month
f. Make specific staff assignments for data collection and analysis and train staff	Two months

Instructions: *Place the letter corresponding to the activity above in the blank below in the Activity column. Draw a time line for the activity.* Hint: *In this case, no activities overlap.*

TIME CHART

Activity	JAN	FEB	MAR	APR	MAY	JUN	JUL	AUG	SEP	OCT
1. _____										
2. _____										
3. _____										
4. _____										
5. _____										
6. _____										

DETERMINING URGENCY AND IMPORTANCE

PROBLEMS FOR ANALYSIS AND DISCUSSION

The following cases are designed to help you think about how you would handle various situations that could occur at work. Study each case and then explain how you think you would handle the situation. Discuss your answers in small groups or with the class as a whole.

Safety Procedures and Regulations

Case 1

You are a troubleshooter (someone who looks for potential problems and makes recommendations on how to handle them) for a manufacturing firm. You are also a liaison (a go-between) between factory supervisors who work on the production line and office managers to whom they report. One day a supervisor for the paint team tells you that three of his workers are not wearing their protective breathing masks because they feel that they are too uncomfortable to wear. Breathing masks filter out small paint particles that float in the air while the painters are spray-painting. State safety regulations require all workers to wear protective masks at all times while painting. If state inspectors were to visit your factory and notice that the painters were not wearing their masks, the company could be fined $1,000 per day for each worker not wearing his or her mask.

Your job is to give advice and make recommendations on how to deal with this problem. State your recommendation below, and explain your reasons for making it.

Case 2

The presses at your company are very powerful and require a worker's full attention so that accidents can be avoided. Safety regulations at your company state that only one employee can work at each mechanical press. You have noticed that workers occasionally ignore this regulation. Sometimes two or three workers will come over to a press worker and begin talking. Doing this is not a violation of state law. However, the rule was established to protect the workers, and it was required by the industrial insurance company that pays for industrial injury claims filed by injured workers. If the insurance company could prove that workers had violated safety procedures, they might not pay an injury claim. State your recommendation to the company for this case and explain your reasons:

Security Procedures

Case 1

Imagine that you are walking through an area of your company that has a sign that says: "EMPLOYEES ONLY." You notice a stranger walking around in the area. You feel reasonably certain that the person is not an employee. Explain how you would handle the situation and explain your reasons:

Case 2

Several days later you are walking through the employee parking lot and see someone breaking into one of the employee's cars. Explain how you would handle this situation and explain your reasons:

Irritating Situations

Sometimes situations that would normally be relatively unimportant can take on more importance. Consider the following cases.

Case 1

You are working in an office shared by four other workers. On this particular day you have a deadline to meet. You feel pressure. It is not, however, a particularly heavy day for the other people in the office. They have been talking about things unrelated to work, telling jokes, and socializing most of the morning. You are having difficulty concentrating. Their conversation is beginning to interfere with your work. Explain how you would deal with this situation and explain your reasons:

Case 2

Your company has an employee parking lot, and in it you have a reserved parking space. One morning as you drive into the parking lot, you notice that another employee from a different department is parked in your space, leaving you nowhere to park. How would you handle this situation? Explain your reasons:

Case 3

Several days later you drive into the parking lot and notice that one of the senior managers has parked in your parking space. Would you handle this situation the same way as in case 2? Explain why you would or would not handle the situation the same way as you did above:

Emergency Situations

Emergencies take precedence over (take on higher priority than) all other issues at hand. Also many rules of routine communication such as concern over using appropriate social register or appropriate tone are generally less important than during normal circumstances. The important rules governing communication during emergencies are to communicate clearly what the nature of the problem is, and to communicate clearly what actions need to be taken. It is also extremely important to communicate in a way that does not create a general panic such as would occur by one's yelling "fire!" in a crowded public place. Much of your effectiveness in communicating during emergency situations is based upon your ability to project the proper degree of seriousness and urgency to others. There is an old story which says that for some people a situation may be hopeless but not serious, whereas for others a situation may be serious but not hopeless. Your attitude will greatly influence how others perceive the situation.

Consider how you would handle the following situations.

Case 1

Your boss has been complaining that she has not been feeling well. You go into her office and see that she is unconscious on the floor. Explain what you would do in this situation and explain your reasons:

Case 2

Your company's main building is being remodeled. You are walking near a construction area when another employee rushes up to you and says that asbestos fibers (a very harmful material if inhaled) are blowing around inside the main office where people are working. How would you handle this situation? Explain your reasons:

FROM THEORY TO PRACTICE: TRYING IT ON YOUR OWN

In order to try out what you have learned, practice the following role-playing situations either in small groups or in front of the class. Those observing should comment on how effectively those in the role-playing exercise perform.

Situation 1: Everyone Is Busy

Three individuals from the group or class should assume roles based upon the cues provided below. In this situation the important thing for the employees to do is not give in until they are certain that the supervisor clearly understands what their work load is. For the supervisor, it is important that he or she make sure someone agrees to do the assignment. Those observing the role play should make notes in the space provided.

PERSON A:

Assume the role of a supervisor. You have just been given an important assignment. The assignment is due by 5:00 P.M. You realize that to

Mark Mangold/U.S. Census Bureau

give it to someone will put the person under pressure, but you have no choice. It will require several hours of hard work.

PERSON B:

Assume the role of an employee who is already busy working on a difficult report that will require most of your time for the next few days. Your work is due Friday, and today is Monday. Your report will take at least three more days to complete. You are not anxious to take on any additional work right now.

PERSON C:

Assume the role of an employee. You have to do daily counts for your section. The counts require about two hours to complete, but occasionally they take a little longer. You are not anxious to take on any additional work right now.

OBSERVER NOTES:

Situation 2: Everyone Wants to Go to Lunch Together

The next situation requires four individuals from the group or class. The important thing for the supervisor to do in this case is to make certain that the phones are covered during lunch. The important thing for the employees to do is work out some type of compromise so that no one employee wil be taken advantage of every day by being the only one who has to stay by the phones while the others go to lunch.

PERSON A:

Assume the role of an office supervisor. You have just received a memo from the division manager stating that during lunch hour at least one employee is to remain in the office to answer the telephones. Consequently, one individual will have to take a late lunch. You have a lunch meeting with the division manager, so you cannot possibly stay during lunch yourself.

PERSONS B, C, AND D:

Assume the roles of office workers who want to go to lunch with the other employees in the office.

OBSERVER NOTES:

Situation 3: Give Me My Parking Space

This role play requires four individuals. The important thing for the facilities supervisor to do is make sure that company rules are followed so that confusion does not rule in the parking lot. The important thing for each employee to do is to clearly express his or her needs.

PERSON A:

Assume the rule of an employee who has just driven into work. Your reserved parking space has been taken by a co-worker whom you know (person B).

PERSON B:

Assume the role of an employee who has just taken a co-worker's (person A) parking space because someone else (person C) has taken your space.

PERSON C:

Assume the role of an employee who has just taken a co-worker's (person B) parking space because you have a large car and so do the people who park on both sides of you; consequently, it is too difficult for you to get out of your car.

PERSON D:

Assume the role of the facilities supervisor. One of your responsibilities is to assign parking spaces.

OBSERVER NOTES:

chapter 6

STYLE AND ATTITUDE
"How Are You Coming Across?"

AFL-CIO News

INTRODUCTION

No matter what kind of organization you work in, large or small, public or private, much of your time will be spent dealing with other people. Some professions, such as counseling or sales, demand greater people contact than others, but virtually no job allows you to hide from the world and its inhabitants. Many students feel that because they are planning to become engineers or accountants they will not need to learn how to get along with others. They are hoping that most of their time will be spent with machines or books and that they won't have to handle "people problems." However, this is only wishful thinking, because even the busiest bookkeeper will sooner or later have to look up from the accounting sheet and deal with the other employees in the company. There is no hiding from other people in any job.

Getting along with other employees, be they superiors, subordinates, or peers, is extremely important for anyone wanting to be successful in his or her work. Studies have shown that one of the main reasons people do not get promoted on the job is that they cannot work well with others. Most organizations realize that no company can afford to have someone in a responsible position who creates friction among the staff. The costs in terms of wasted energy, bad will, and decreased productivity would be too great.

For many employees, dealing effectively with their fellow employees is often the most difficult part of the job. They may ask themselves: "How do I react to a boss who is a tough guy and loves to yell and scream at his subordinates? How do I handle a co-worker who constantly complains about everything or a Pollyanna who refuses to acknowledge problems?"

In addition to not being able to figure out how to respond to the style of others, many people have trouble determining how their own behavior is interpreted by those around them. They are not certain how they are coming across to others and often are not even sure whether or not their fellow employees like them. They may think that they are being pleasant and agreeable when in fact they are perceived as being superfriendly. Superfriendlies are people who are so concerned about getting along with others that they do so at the expense of getting work done. Or they may pride themselves on being well-liked because they are easygoing and willing to compromise when in fact they are driving their co-workers crazy by acting wishy-washy and indecisive.

The way we are perceived by others is called *style*, and the positive or negative response we bring to a situation is called *attitude*. Style and attitude determine whether we are seen as cooperative by the rest of the organization, or whether we are termed "troublemakers." Being able to analyze and adapt your own style and developing strategies for understanding and dealing with the styles of others are probably the most valuable nontechnical skills you can attain at work.

VOCABULARY CHECK

Match each of the following terms with the numbered phrase that best explains the concept.

_____ a. virtually

_____ b. wishful thinking

_____ c. decreased productivity

_____ d. tough guy

_____ e. Pollyanna

_____ f. wishy-washy

_____ g. "superfriendlies"

_____ h. indecisive

_____ i. style

_____ j. attitude

1. a way of behaving that is typical of that person
2. practically, almost without exception
3. not being able to make up one's mind
4. colloquial for indecisive
5. a person who will only see the positive aspects of a situation and refuses to admit that anything bad could happen
6. someone who pretends he has no weaknesses; someone who shouts at people and bosses them around
7. people who are more concerned about being well-liked by everyone than about getting their work done
8. a slowdown in the work produced and the tasks accomplished; less output
9. the positive or negative responses you have to a particular situation
10. the hope that things will turn out the way you want them to in spite of evidence to the contrary

QUESTIONS FOR DISCUSSION

1. Name some jobs that require a great deal of contact with other people.

2. Name some jobs where employees don't have to deal with other people.

3. What are some reasons why employees do not get promoted?

4. What are some of the types of co-workers that can make getting along at work difficult?

5. What do we mean when we say that someone has a Pollyanna attitude? Give an example.

6. What problems would a superfriendly person have? How are such people perceived by their superiors?

7. How do wishy-washy people often see themselves?

8. What do style and attitude determine?

TYPES OF STYLES

Since the time we were small, we have developed certain ways of communicating and interacting with other people. We have learned to use those strategies that allow us to achieve the results we want. We have also learned to avoid those methods that seem to be counterproductive. In other words, we have developed our own style. Although most of us are not so set in our ways that others can predict how we will act in a given situation, many people have a clear style of their own that can be characterized by certain behavior patterns. Look at the styles discussed below and see if you know anyone who would fit that particular style. As you do this, remember that these are stereotypes (overgeneralizations). These labels rarely fit any one person's behavior exactly.

The Superfriendlies

Superfriendlies try to get along with everyone and try to be nice at all costs. They do not make trouble and get very nervous when they see people arguing or fighting. They value relationships above all else and are quite willing to sacrifice achievement for harmony. They go out of their way to maintain peace in a group even if it is a false peace.

They will often allow themselves to be exploited and will not speak up even if accused unjustly. They cannot deal with the idea that someone may

Ken Karp

not like them or even be mad at them. They are quite willing to give up their own desires and give in to the desires of others as long as it means acceptance by the group. Their motto is "Peace at any cost."

The Tough Guys

Tough guys (which includes women as well as men) enjoy a good fight and love to argue about problems and issues. When they have their mind set on accomplishing a particular achievement, they work toward that goal with a single-minded effort that astounds their co-workers. They sacrifice a great deal to be a winner. It does not matter to them whether other people like them or agree with their tactics. In their struggle for power, they show very little concern for the feelings of others and often yell or shout when things don't go their way. They seldom regret sacrificing friendships for success. Their motto is: "Winning isn't the only thing. It's everything."

Ken Karp

The Experts

Experts set themselves up as authorities on any matter—technical, social, or political. They seem to have all the answers and enjoy giving advice and making suggestions. They are very happy to give advice on any problem and do not mind sharing their vast knowledge with their co-workers. Their motto is: "Ask me anything; I'll give you the answer."

The Logical Problem Solvers

Logical problem solvers concentrate on tasks instead of on people. Often they don't understand why some employees are having problems with each other. To the logical problem solvers, emotional problems are not "real" and feelings don't matter in a business environment. They prefer to see all problems from an intellectual point of view and try to find a logical solution to any conflict. Their motto is: "There seems to be no logical basis for emotional conflict."

The Pessimists

Pessimists always expect the worst. They don't believe in luck and try to prepare for negative results. They dampen spirits when co-workers start to get excited about an idea or when enthusiasm runs high. Generally they would not be surprised if the company went out of business and everyone got fired. Their motto is: "It won't work."

The Pollyannas

Pollyannas look at the world through rose-colored glasses. They keep hoping that everything will turn out well despite many signs to the contrary. They try to keep morale high by telling everyone that things will get better. They tend to smile a lot. They are sure that they will be happy and successful even if they don't deserve to be. Their motto is: "It'll all work out. No problem."

The Complainers

Complainers enjoy griping. Nothing is ever good enough for them. In their mind, all the bosses are too demanding and the company is trying to cheat everyone. They complain that co-workers are either too lazy and not carrying their load or compulsive about work and trying to impress their superiors. The temperature in their office is either too hot or too cold and the food in the cafeteria is never edible. Their motto is: "This place stinks."

The Indecisive

Indecisive people have a hard time making up their minds. They put off making any decision for fear it might be the wrong one. When given a new responsibility, they continue to ask everyone for advice long after they should have mastered the task. They are so afraid of making a mistake that they will take forever to finish a project. Their motto is: "You can't be too careful."

The Middle of the Roaders

Middle of the roaders look for the middle ground in any conflict. They try to find a compromise for any position and feel that no matter what the situation, each side should be gaining something. Often as a result of these compromises, neither group wins anything and both may lose.

QUESTIONS FOR DISCUSSION

1. What are some of the advantages of being a "superfriendly"?

2. What are some of the disadvantages?

3. Why is it difficult to deal with "tough guys"?

4. What happens if you ask an "expert" for advice?

5. How does a "logical problem solver" deal with people's emotional problems?

6. What is the motto of the pessimists?

7. How do "Pollyannas" see the world?

8. What do complainers think of their bosses, their work, and their co-workers?

9. Why can't the "indecisive" make up their minds?

PROBLEMS FOR ANALYSIS AND DISCUSSION

Answer the following questions about the styles discussed in the previous section. Then compare your answers with those of your classmates and explain your opinion. See if your group can come to a consensus.

1. Which style would be the most effective in a business setting? Which would be the most effective in a social setting? Explain.

2. Which style would be the most destructive in a business setting? How about a social setting? Explain.

3. Which style would be considered the most effective or most appropriate for a business setting/social setting in your culture? Explain.

4. Which style comes closest to your own? Which style is the most prevalent (common) in your family? Explain.

5. Which styles could be combined for an effective approach to handling problems at work? Explain.

6. If you could choose the types of colleagues you wanted to work with, what types would you choose? Explain.

7. Which types would you find the most difficult to work with? Explain.

8. Which type of boss would you prefer to have? Explain.

9. What type of person would you refuse to work for? Explain.

10. What types of people would you like to have as subordinates? Explain.

11. What types of employees would you fire? Explain.

12. If you had a middle of the roader and two tough guys working together, what would be the result?

MANAGING YOUR OWN STYLE

There is no one perfect style that everyone should try to maintain under all circumstances. Most styles have positive as well as negative aspects to them. For example, a "tough guy" may not be popular with his subordinates at the office, but he is often appreciated by management for his ability to make decisions and get important work done. Thus, the same style that makes his subordinates dislike him may earn him praise from his superiors.

For most people, the advantages and disadvantages of a particular style balance each other out. However, there are some people who have become so inflexible in their responses that a style that could be a personal strength ends up as a weakness. Take the example of the supervisor who was well-liked by all of her employees because she was consistently nice and accommodating. Unfortunately, she remained nice and accommodating even when some of her staff took advantage of her good-heartedness by making personal long distance phone calls, taking two-hour lunches, and

Courtesy U.S. Census Bureau

balancing their checkbooks on company time. As time went on, the supervisor not only lost all of the respect her staff had had for her, she lost her job as well!

As the case of the superfriendly supervisor shows, an overplayed strength can easily become a weakness. To avoid getting stuck in a rigid pattern, it is important for employees to learn how to adjust their language and behavior to the circumstances so that their style can work *for* them rather than *against* them.

QUESTIONS FOR DISCUSSION

1. Which is considered the perfect style?

2. Why does management often appreciate a "tough guy"?

3. Give an example of a personal strength becoming a weakness.

4. If a supervisor appears weak, what can be the result as far as his or her subordinates are concerned?

5. What should your personal style do for you?

PROBLEMS FOR ANALYSIS AND DISCUSSION

The following cases are designed to help you determine how different people with different styles would approach a problem. After you have decided how each person would act and what he or she might say, try to determine what the results would be as far as the work situation is concerned. Discuss your ideas with the rest of the class.

Case 1

A supervisor is in charge of a group of people who are working under a deadline. The company is preparing an important proposal (sixty pages), which must be in the mail by five o'clock. It is three o'clock and the proposal pages still need to be proofread, photocopied (eight copies), collated, and mailed. Alan, an older clerk, was borrowed from another department for the afternoon so that he could help the staff get the proposal ready. Unfortunately, he has a dentist appointment at 3:30. Alan explains that he has to leave and points out that his dentist is a very busy woman so it would be difficult to get another appointment with her soon.

The supervisor now needs to decide whether to let Alan go or to insist that he stay on the job. Decide how supervisors with different styles would handle the situation.

1. How would an optimist handle the situation? What would he say?

2. How would a tough guy handle the situation? What would he say?

3. How would a superfriendly person handle this situation?

4. How would a middle of the roader handle the situation?

5. How would a problem solver handle the situation?

6. How would an indecisive person handle the situation?

7. How would you handle the situation?

Case 2

Jenny is a new employee in a small firm. She likes most of the people she works with, but there is one employee, Beth, whose style bothers her. Beth is a very warm person who likes to show the affection she feels for her colleagues by touching them briefly or by occasionally giving them a quick hug. When she talks to Jenny, she sometimes pats her on the back or puts her arm around her for a few seconds. Jenny is a very shy person, and any type of physical contact from nonfamily members bothers her. How should she deal with her co-worker's style? Rank the choices below from 1 to 6 (1 is best). Be prepared to discuss your answers (for number 7, explain how you would handle the situation).

_____ 1. Jenny should be forceful and aggressive and tell Beth in no uncertain terms that she hates to be touched. If Beth tries touching her again, Jenny should push her away.

_____ 2. Jenny should just forget about it and relax. Beth is just trying to be friendly; Jenny shouldn't be so nervous.

_____ 3. Jenny should start by trying to send nonverbal messages; that is, she should move her shoulder when Beth pats her and move away slightly when Beth leans toward her.

_____ 4. Jenny should immediately report Beth to the supervisor. Touching other employees is not appropriate in a work setting and Beth should be told so.

_____ 5. Jenny should wait until she sees Beth at break time or at another relaxing occasion and bring up the fact that because of her cultural background she is not comfortable being touched. She should try to assure her co-worker that that doesn't mean she doesn't like her.

_____ 6. Jenny should reverse the situation by touching the woman every chance she gets. This would teach Beth a lesson and show her how uncomfortable it can feel to be touched.

_____ 7. Other. Explain how you would handle the situation differently.

Case 3

Minh works as a painter in a truck plant. His boss is a rough person who often loses his temper and yells at the workers. Minh has to wear a protective safety mask when he paints; he knows he is also supposed to put the mask in a special bin when he is done so that it can be cleaned. One evening Minh is in a rush to go home and puts his mask in his locker instead. When his boss sees the next morning that Minh is putting on a mask that has not been cleaned, he blows up. He tells Minh that he is stupid and irresponsible and threatens to report him. How should Minh deal with his boss? Rank the choices below from 1 to 6 (1 is best). Be prepared to discuss your answers (for number 7, explain how you would handle the situation).

_____ 1. Minh should quit. He shouldn't work in a place where he is being yelled at and treated like a child.

_____ 2. Minh should calmly explain to his boss that he does not like being yelled at and ask him not to do it anymore.

_____ 3. Minh should forget about the incident and follow work rules from now on.

_____ 4. Minh should try to get his boss to change his ways. He should tell him to take things easy and relax more so that he won't lose his temper as easily.

_____ 5. Minh should give his boss some of his own medicine and yell at him the next time his supervisor makes a mistake. That would show his boss how unpleasant it can be to be yelled at.

_____ 6. Minh should take his complaint to the union. The unions are set up to mediate problems between workers and management. A union representative will talk to Minh's boss for him.

_____ 7. Other. Explain how you would handle the situation.

FROM THEORY TO PRACTICE: TRYING IT ON YOUR OWN_____

Look at the following cases and decide how you would handle each situation. Next, choose a partner and role-play the situation. Then analyze what style each person used.

Laimute E. Druskis

1. One of the people in your company is retiring and there will be a farewell party. A co-worker, who is a pretty tough guy, comes to you and asks you if you could please be in charge of the dinner and the entertainment. You know that there will be a lot of work that needs to be done. How much are you willing to do, and how far will you allow yourself to be pushed?

2. You and a co-worker are talking about the general condition of the economy. You are trying to decide what jobs will be available in the future and what will happen to the standard of living. Discuss the future of the economy with others.

3. You are working for a bank that is trying to decide whether all employees who deal with customers should be wearing uniforms. The bank has decided to leave the decision up to the employees. There are strong opinions on both sides of this issue. Work in a group and take a position.

4. One of your co-workers is a complainer; he complains about how tough the boss is and how inconsiderate all his co-workers are (give examples). Respond to the complaints.

5. You are thinking of purchasing a new car, but you are not sure which kind to buy. You are bringing up the idea at lunch time. Discuss the idea with two fellow workers.

chapter 7

RESUME WRITING:
Presenting Yourself on Paper

Rhoda Sidney/Monkmeyer Press

INTRODUCTION

For many jobs, especially professional jobs, it is necessary to have a resume and to keep it up-to-date. Resumes are used not only to get your first job or when you are trying to change jobs; they can also be used when you are seeking a promotion or new position in a company where you are already employed. Or, if you are going to be assigned to work on a federal or state contract, you may be asked for a copy of your resume in order to show the federal or state monitors that you are qualified to work on the project.

Because many people lack the confidence to write their own resumes, they pay to have their resumes professionally written. In this chapter we will show you several simple steps you can use to write your own resume. Since you may need to write and rewrite your resume many times during your career, we suggest that you learn how to do it yourself. After all, who knows your background and qualifications better than you?

There are a number of resume styles. One of the most common types is a _chronological_ resume. A chronological resume provides a general picture of your experience and background in reverse chronological order, listing your most recent experience first. Another common type of resume is a _functional_ resume. Functional resumes emphasize your most important assets while deemphasizing chronological order. Both approaches have their strong points. You should choose a style that best presents your background and qualifications. No single style is best for all situations. In fact, often it is advisable to combine some aspects of the functional resume with aspects of the chronological resume in order to strengthen your overall image.

In terms of length, your resume should be concise yet long enough to cover the highlights of your background that are significant. It may need to be several pages in length. However, it is not a good idea to "pad" your resume with many insignificant details, especially if they are not relevant to the job for which you are applying.

Writing a resume helps you analyze your background in terms of all your strengths. If you have some years of experience related to the job for which you are applying, it is important that you summarize that experience. On the other hand, if you are a young person, you may not have had extensive paid experience. Perhaps you have gained valuable experience through volunteer activities or through training. Generally, the more you analyze your background, the more you will be surprised by the qualifications that you do have.

SELF-ASSESSMENT

Before you can write a resume or do well in an employment interview, it is necessary for you to do some assessment of your skills, experience, training, and special qualities that would be of interest to a potential employer. In this section we will identify aspects of your background that are easily overlooked. The main trick is to identify skills that you have and to represent them in terms that will be meaningful to potential employers.

Using Action Words to Describe Your Background

How many times have you been asked the question, "What do you do for a living?" There is a tendency for people to answer this question by saying, for example, "I'm an engineer" or "I'm a salesman." In everyday conversations these answers are acceptable, but in an interview the interviewer will be more interested in your skills than in your former titles. On your resume you must try to put more emphasis on things you can do and have done rather than on what you are or were called while doing those things. In order to signal what you can do and what you have done, it is useful to think of your skills and experience in terms of action verbs. Action verbs are words like *build, develop, evaluate,* and so on. The use of these verbs in your resume will help you to present yourself as a doer rather than a sitter.

Examples of Action Verbs

build	manage	promote	assess
construct	oversee	negotiate	analyze
provide	supervise	sell	evaluate
maintain	coordinate	market	interpret
organize	assist	sponsor	examine
operate	teach	facilitate	review
assemble	instruct	expedite	critique
design	train	advocate for	proof
develop	counsel	represent	troubleshoot

Which verbs apply specifically to you? Try to answer the following questions using some of the verbs just listed.

- What work have you previously done?
- What skills were involved?
- What types of duties did you have?
- What relationships with people were involved?
- What responsibilities did you have?

Discovering Transferable Skills

Often what we learn in one line of work is transferable to another. With the vocabulary of a resume, we can signal transferable skills by using action verbs.

Study the following example from a resume; try to determine what position this person had by studying the action verbs that are used to describe the work done.

Example

Work Experience

- *prepared* daily deliveries
- *delivered* on a daily basis to customers
- *maintained* accounts on customers
- *collected* customer fees on a monthly basis
- *solicited* new subscriptions
- *responded* to customer complaints and concerns

Have you guessed what this person does? If you guessed newspaper delivery, then you have guessed correctly. As you can see, the trick is to take whatever skills you have and to present them in a positive light. Of course this can be carried too far, but generally most people have had more transferable experience than they realize.

Obviously, a position in newspaper delivery will not provide you with transferable experience for most jobs, but as you analyze the activities listed above, which ones do you think are transferable? In what types of work would these activities be useful as experience?

VOCABULARY CHECK

Match each of the following terms with the numbered phrase below that best explains the concept. Note: *Only seven answers are correct.*

_____ a. resume

_____ b. chronological resume

_____ c. functional resume

_____ d. self-assessment

_____ e. background

_____ f. experience

_____ g. action verbs

1. what you have learned through the work you have done
2. words that make you sound important
3. words that make you appear to be a "doer"
4. your education, training, and work history
5. a brief summary of your skills and qualifications
6. an analysis of your background to determine skills and characteristics that are of interest to employers
7. a brief time-sequenced summary of your skills and qualifications
8. a resume that emphasizes your most important achievements rather than the order of their occurrence
9. an analysis of the job market

QUESTIONS FOR DISCUSSION

1. What is a functional resume?
2. What is a chronological resume?
3. Which type of resume is better? Explain.
4. What is meant by padding a resume? Is it a good idea to do so?
5. Is it all right to put volunteer experience on your resume if you have not previously had a lot of experience? Explain.
6. What are action verbs? Give several examples.
7. Why should you use action verbs on your resume?
8. What are transferable skills?

PROBLEMS FOR ANALYSIS AND DISCUSSION

Case 1

Imagine that you have been asked to help a farmer construct a resume. The farmer owned his farm for fifteen years and is now forced to change fields. Consequently, he will need to analyze skills he has acquired that are transferable. Analyze the farmer's experience in terms of the types of skills he has acquired. In answering the following questions, list his skills by using *action verbs* that apply to what he has done.

1. Who does the farmer have to deal with in order to grow his product? Does he need to hire people or cooperate with other farmers? If so, what skills in dealing with people does he need?

   Example: *hires* temporary workers, *negotiates* work agreements

2. What type of business is the farmer running?

   Example: *owns, operates,* and *manages* Greenfield Farm

3. What financial dealings does a farmer have? Does he borrow money? If so, what skills does he need in order to get a loan?

   Example: *estimates* annual expenditures, *negotiates* loans

Now try to complete the following on your own.

4. What financial record does the farmer maintain?
5. What planning skills does a farmer need?
6. What machines does a farmer need to operate?
7. What organizational skills does a farmer need?
8. What skills does a farmer need in order to sell what he grows?

Case 2

Consider the case of a student who has had little or no paid experience. What skills acquired in daily academic life are likely to be transferable to most employment situations?

Under each question below, list several action verbs that represent transferable skills. Next, discuss your answers and your reasons for them.

1. What oral communication skills has a student generally acquired?
2. What writing skills has a student generally acquired?
3. What analytical/problem-solving skills has a student usually acquired?
4. What types of responsibility has a student usually had to develop both in terms of academic life and in terms of personal life (managing personal finances and so on)?
5. What types of deadlines has a student often had to meet? Or, what types of pressure has a student frequently had to work under?
6. What types of practical skills, training, and knowledge has a student generally acquired through his or her classes?

ANALYZING YOUR OWN BACKGROUND BY USING THE ADVANCE RESUME ORGANIZER

The exercise that follows requires you to analyze your own background in terms of skills, qualifications, experience, and so on. To help you do this, we have provided an advance resume organizer, which breaks down your background in terms of specific questions.

Advance Resume Organizer

Briefly answer the following questions.

1. What education background do you have? (List schools attended, dates enrolled, diplomas and degrees, major field or area of study.)

Mimi Forsyth/Monkmeyer Press

2. What work or employment experiences have you had? (List both paid and unpaid or volunteer experience; list dates and place of experience.)

3. What kind of special training have you had? (List specialized training programs or experiences that you may have had.)

4. What special licenses or certificates do you have? (List them and indicate dates received.)

5. What languages do you read, speak, or write? (List them and indicate your degree of fluency.)

6. What hobbies or special interests do you have?

7. What types of machines or special equipment do you know how to operate? (For typing or word processing indicate your average speed; also list whatever computers you know how to work with, what computer languages you know, and what types of software you can use.)

8. What special awards or recognition have you received? (Indicate the specific name of the award, the date received, and who gave it to you.)

9. What experiences in supervising, managing, or coordinating people have you had? (List both paid and volunteer experiences.)

10. What financial skills do you have? (List experiences in doing budgets, collecting money, etc.)

11. List any other skills or abilities you may have.

12. What job or position are you looking for?

TIPS ON RESUME WRITING

Resume writing involves choices about how you want to present yourself. Below you will find suggestions related to presenting your background in the best possible way.

What Should Be Emphasized: Chronological Order or Order of Importance?

When you write your resume, you have a choice between listing your information in chronological order or reverse chronological order. Since most people tend to advance in their careers, reverse chronological is usually better because it places emphasis on your most recent achievements. Sometimes, however, if you have held more than one job at a time or have had interruptions in your work experience, it may be better to list your information according to "best first" arrangement. In other words, list your most important information first and try to downplay your chronological references.

What If There Are Time Gaps in Your Resume?

If there are large time gaps between items of information, be prepared to explain why these gaps are there, because you may be questioned about them in an interview.

Should You Include Negative Information in Your Resume?

Avoid putting negative information in your resume. A resume is not a public confession. If information is requested on an application, it is necessary to include it, but on a resume you have some choice regarding what you want to include or ignore.

How Much Should You Include in Your Resume?

Try not to pad your resume with unnecessary details that do not relate to the job. On the other hand, if you have been active in service activities, community organizations, or sports, especially team sports, you may want to include that type of information. Employers are especially interested in how you will fit socially into the workplace; this type of information indicates that you probably like people and can get along with others.

What Things Should You Emphasize First: Education, Training, or Experience?

If you have had little on-the-job experience related to your employment objective, you will probably want to emphasize your education and training. However, it is still a good idea to include some evidence of work experience even if it is not directly related to your objective. Most employers like to see some evidence that you have had the experience of working with others. If your previous experience is unrelated to your objective, be prepared to explain why you have changed fields. If you have worked for a few years in your particular field, you may wish to emphasize your experience first, since that has now became your strongest proof that you can do the job. Education, however, is still important and may demonstrate to your employer the depth of your overall background.

Should You Include Names of Personal References?

A common procedure is to include a statement such as: "References available upon request" or "References on file at the Office of Career Planning and Development at [list the name of your school's office if you have one]." Generally, you should not include names on your resume.

CHOOSING PERSONAL REFERENCES

Personal references can be an important part of getting a job. Consequently you should choose your personal references carefully. Make sure that the person you choose knows your qualifications well enough to give you a positive recommendation without hesitation or uncertainty. Do not just choose someone who likes you. Make sure the person you select can explain what your job-related qualifications are. Choose someone who has the authority to evaluate your job qualifications. Finally, check with the person in advance and discuss with him or her what your objectives are; ask permission to use this person as a reference. Ask your reference person to explain what type of recommendation he or she would feel comfortable giving.

EXERCISE

List three individuals whom you feel could give you a good recommendation. Next state what relationship you have had with each person. Then, explain why you are sure this person is qualified to give you a good recommendation.

1. Name:

   Relationship:

   Reason for choosing this reference:

2. Name:

   Relationship:

   Reason for choosing this reference:

3. Name:

   Relationship:

   Reason for choosing this reference:

STATING YOUR EMPLOYMENT OBJECTIVES AND SUMMARIZING YOUR SKILLS AND QUALIFICATIONS

There are basically two views among employment specialists regarding employment objectives. Many employment specialists feel that a statement of employment objectives is too specific and may actually limit your employment opportunities. Generally this may be true for those entering the job market for the first time. Other employment specialists argue that your resume should be tailored for the specific job for which you are applying. Thus, they say if you know the specific field or position for which you are applying, you should include a brief section near the top of your resume similar to the following:

> **EMPLOYMENT OBJECTIVE:** Seeking a responsible position as a marketing analyst with opportunity for advancement.

NOTE: You may also use "Job Objective" or "Career Objective" as headings for this type of statement.

The trick here is to make sure the statement is broad enough to show flexibility but specific enough to emphasize areas in which you would be interested in working. If you are not sure about what specific position you are going for (and wish the prospective employer to keep your resume on file in case it may be reviewed for a general field rather than for a specific position), you may wish to include a brief introductory statement as a summary of your skills. An example of a summary statement is the following:

> **SUMMARY OF SKILLS AND QUALIFICATIONS:** Extensive experience and training in market analysis and market research. Analytical and research skills have allowed me to achieve success within a major computer corporation.

NOTE: You may also use "Qualifications" or "Background" as headings for this type of statement.

Long-term Versus Short-term Employment Objectives

As you write your employment objectives, it is a good idea to give some thought as to whether your objectives are short term or long term. For example, your long-term objective may be to become president of the company, but don't try listing that as an immediate objective if you are seeking an entry-level position.

Following are examples of a short-term job objective and a long-term career objective:

JOB OBJECTIVE: Seeking a summer position in which my skills in engineering and computer science may be applied to problem solving and analysis.

CAREER OBJECTIVE: Seeking a career in research and development in aerospace with an opportunity for steadily increasing responsibility and advancement.

EXERCISE

1. Write one sentence that explains what your employment objectives are. Assume you are writing for a specific position.

2. Write one or two sentences summarizing your skills and qualifications.

3. Write a short-term job objective.

4. Write a long-term career objective.

FROM THEORY TO PRACTICE: TRYING IT ON YOUR OWN

Draft Your Own Resume

Now try to draft a resume. Refer to the Resume Organizer to help guide you. Refer to the Advance Resume Organizer exercise to determine the major areas you should consider. Refer to the list of Action Verbs to help you determine what types of verbs you should list under each job title. You may also refer to the sample resumes at the end of this chapter.

As you study the sample resumes, note that there is some flexibility in style, format, and titles of headings. The format presented in the Resume Organizer is meant to be suggestive. Again, the final arrangement you choose will be based on your particular background. For example, if you have more qualifications related to education than to work experience, you will want to list your education first. If you are applying for a particular job, you may wish to use the heading "Employment Objective" rather than "Summary of Skills and Qualifications."

Note that the Resume Organizer suggests various subheadings commonly found on resumes. These are not the only headings (or format style) that may be used. Regardless of which headings or format you choose, make sure that your resume is neat, is logical, and can be easily understood by someone who is not familiar with your background.

RESUME ORGANIZER

Name (Family name last)

Address

Telephone Number

(If you are applying for a specific job, use the following:)

EMPLOYMENT OBJECTIVE: *I am seeking a responsible position as a . . .*

(If you are writing a general resume but are not applying for a specific position, use the following:)

SUMMARY OF SKILLS AND QUALIFICATIONS: *Extensive experience in . . .*

EDUCATION: (List your highest degree first; then follow with the next highest, and so on.)

(*WHAT:* Degree/diploma/certificate)

(*WHERE:* School/institute)

(*WHEN:* Date of completion)

WORK EXPERIENCE:

(*WHO:* Position/title)

(*WHERE:* Name of place/institution where you performed your work)

(*WHAT* did you do? List action verbs and brief explanations of what you did on the job.)

(*WHEN* did you do this? List starting date to termination date.)

SPECIAL SKILLS/TRAINING:

(Have you had special training through specialty schools, through the military, or through in-service training?)

(Do you have special licenses or certificates?) If you have, list *WHAT* it is, *WHERE* you received it, *WHEN* you received it, and for *HOW LONG* it is valid.)

Resume Organizer
Page 2

SPECIAL AWARDS:

(Have you received any special honors and/or awards? *WHAT* type of award/honor was it? *WHERE* was it awarded? *BY WHOM* was it awarded?)

LANGUAGE SKILLS:

(*WHICH* languages do you speak, read, or write? Indicate your degree of fluency. List only if fluent.)

REFERENCES AVAILABLE UPON REQUEST

(Add this phrase, but do not list your references by name.)

(*NOTE:* Age, sex, race, and marital status are not necessary.)

SAMPLE RESUME
OF A COLLEGE STUDENT

RESUME

Jon Martois
2247 Pine Avenue, Apt. 4
Pima Vista, Arizona 70233
Telephone (267) 987-1254

Seeking a position as an Engineering Assistant where I can apply the practical and analytical skills learned in college and where I can gain experience related to my career objectives in Civil Engineering.

EDUCATION

1/87–Present   University of Arizona, Tucson, Arizona

Progressing toward a Bachelor of Science Degree in Civil Engineering (expected 1991). Practical training includes field work in surveying and map reading, computer programming in BASIC and PASCAL.

9/83–6/86   St. Luke's Preparatory Institute, Paris, France

Diploma (6/86). College preparatory studies. Class rank: 5th in class of 107 students. Voted Outstanding Science Student.

WORK EXPERIENCE

8/86–Present   Circle Q Market, Tucson, Arizona

As Night Manager, responsible for maintaining stock, supervising two clerks, scheduling work assignments, serving customers, making deposits, and closing out. This position pays for most of my college living expenses.

HOBBIES

Rock hunting and collecting, hiking, and cross-country skiing.

LANGUAGES

Fluent in French, fairly good in English, some Spanish.

*   *   *   REFERENCES PROVIDED UPON REQUEST   *   *   *

PROBLEMS FOR GROUP DISCUSSION

Study Jon Martois's resume. Answer the following questions. Fully explain your answers and be prepared to discuss them.

1. Does Jon have a summary of skills and qualifications or a job objective? Which do you feel is best in his case? Explain.

2. Why do you think Jon did not include his current grade point average (GPA)?

3. Do you feel that he should have included the information about his high school education? Explain.

4. How do you feel about the way he has presented his work experience? Is it related to the job he is applying for? Does it help or hurt his chances of getting the job? Explain.

5. Are Jon's hobbies relevant or related to the job for which he is applying? Explain.

6. How do you feel about the way in which Jon has handled his language ability? Explain.

SAMPLE RESUME OF A RECENT CIVIL ENGINEERING GRADUATE

RESUME

Susan Lee
2745 E. 75th Street
Marston, MD 20879
(301) 555-6798

EMPLOYMENT OBJECTIVE

Seeking an entry-level position with a private company or governmental agency that will provide an opportunity to gain experience and responsibility.

EDUCATION

Master of Science Degree in Civil Engineering, University of Maryland (1986). Specialization: Toxic Waste Disposal and Environmental Problems. GPA 3.7.

Bachelor of Science Degree in Civil Engineering, University of Maryland (1983). Honors: Dean's List last four semesters. GPA 3.4.

PRACTICAL EXPERIENCE

Assisted on university research project, "Alternative Methods of Toxic Waste Containment and Disposal." Made field observations and assisted Project Coordinator in formalizing recommendations.

WORK EXPERIENCE

GRADUATE ASSISTANT, University of Maryland (1985–86).
Graded lab reports, assisted professors in counseling undergraduate students.

NIGHT MANAGER, Garden Shop, National Department Store, Inc. (1983–84)
Supervised three salespeople, maintained and ordered stock, handled customer complaints.

COMPUTER LANGUAGES

BASIC, FORTRAN, PASCAL, and COBOL

EXTRACURRICULAR ACTIVITIES

Swim team (1980–82) and Computer Club (1985–86)

PROBLEMS FOR GROUP DISCUSSION

Study Susan Lee's resume carefully and try to answer the following questions. Fully explain your answers and be prepared to discuss them.

1. Which aspect of Susan's resume represents her strongest qualification, her education or her work experience?

2. Why do you think Susan added the section titled "Practical Experience"?

3. Susan does not indicate if her practical experience was paid or unpaid. Do you think she should volunteer that information?

4. Susan listed her grade point averages. Was that a good idea?

5. Is it a good idea to list extracurricular activities such as those that Susan has listed?

6. Do you feel anything is missing that Susan could have listed but did not?

7. Is Susan's resume a functional resume, a chronological resume, or a combination of the two?

8. Would you give Susan an interview on the basis of her resume if you were a personnel manager?

SAMPLE RESUME OF A MIDCAREER PROFESSIONAL

RESUME

Arnold Alfuad
522 Hartford Street
New York, NY 10017

EDUCATION: M.S., Electrical Engineering, Purdue University, 1965
B.S., Electrical Engineering, Purdue University, 1963

GENERAL BACKGROUND: Department Staff Engineer, presently employed in aerospace industry. Capable of leading development effort in analog and digital electronics design; responsible for development of microprocessor-based digital avionics and test equipment; extensive experience in Intel 8050 and 8086 microprocessor systems.

PROFESSIONAL EXPERIENCE:

1982 to Present: PGR DEFENSE AND SPACE SYSTEMS GROUP, SANDY BEACH, NY

WORK PACKAGE MANAGER: Oversee the development of the 200 Mbps digital data multiplexer subsystem for satellite communication system.

Responsibilities include system design, coordination, and supervision of engineering team in the development of the 400 Mhz clock generator and high-speed analog to digital data conversion subsystems. Prepared 200 Mbps cryptic key generator proposal for a Wideband Privacy System military satellite communication. Prepared and presented design reviews. Management tasks include generation of project work authorization, cost estimates, detailed tasks planning and schedules.

1979 to 1982: COLLINS GOVERNMENT AVIONICS, BOSWELL INTERNATIONAL, NEWPORT BEACH, CA

SENIOR PROJECT ENGINEER: Responsible for development of high-speed fiber optic MIL-STD's 1533 multiplexed database system for military avionics systems; managed development project for the development of multilevel multiplexed Information Transfer System to interconnect advanced avionics subsystems, and integration of the radar and omnidirectional air data system for the U.S. Coast Guard HH-65A helicopter.

Arnold Alfuad
Page 2

PROFESSIONAL EXPERIENCE (continued):

1972 to 1979 LUGHES AIRCRAFT COMPANY, EL SEGUNDO, CA

PROJECT ENGINEER: Managed development project for the design and development of instrumentation system for advanced technology radar system, using microprocessor technology; designed automatic data reduction hardware with Intel 8050 microprocessor systems; responsible for system development of modular programmable digital signal processor with distributive microprocessor network system approach, using AM 2901 microprocessors. Have also had direct development experience in microprogrammed systems and sophisticated applications, including the Intellec MDS and Series II microcomputer development systems and the 8085A assembly language and microprogramming techniques. With knowledge of microprocessor technology, ability to interface with private industries.

1970 to 1972: INNOVATION ELECTRIC COMPANY, FRANKLIN PARK, IL

PRODUCT ENGINEER: Responsible for design and development of automatic testing systems for telephone repeaters and high-voltage protection devices. System design phase included development of automatic testing systems to perform multitudes of tests on telephone repeaters and protection devices. Interface circuit design phase included the development of a multichannel BCD scanner, analog-to-digital converters, and various peripheral interface circuits.

1967 to 1970: PALMO RICTOR COMPANY, BELMONT, CA

STAFF ENGINEER: Engaged in the design of both active and passive RF circuits; responsible for design and analysis of RF signal processor for phase lock receivers and transponders; developed computer analysis of phase lock receiver tracking error and stability; designed RF receiver front-end, solid-state RF amplifiers, and various RF subsystems; preparation of proposals for F-14 ECM systems.

1965 to 1967: HOLBERG ELECTRIC COMPANY, COLUMBUS, IND

ELECTRICAL ENGINEER: Developed a program to synthesize an industrial electrical control system.

PROBLEMS FOR GROUP DISCUSSION

Study Arnold Alfuad's resume. Answer the following questions. Fully explain your answers and be prepared to discuss them.

1. Why has education been so greatly reduced in emphasis compared with the emphasis that it received on Susan Lee's resume?

2. Is the section called "General Background" similar to a Job Objective or to a Summary of Skills and Qualifications?

3. Do you think Alfuad is writing for a personnel manager who has a general background, or for a manager who has a technical background?

4. Do you think Alfuad's many jobs show that he has a strong background, or do they indicate that he does not seem to be able to keep a job?

5. Do you think that Alfuad's language is too technical or about right?

6. Is any significant information missing from this resume?

7. Is Alfuad's resume a functional resume or a chronological resume?

8. If you were a personnel manager in Electrical Engineering, would you give Alfuad an interview based on his resume?

SAMPLE RESUME OF A MIDCAREER PROFESSIONAL

RESUME

Sun Soo Chen
618 Johnston Street
Garden Grove, California 92645
Telephone (714) 992-1138

Extensive experience in computer programming, systems programming, and management for production and sales, with interest in a position with growth potential.

EDUCATION

Master of Science Degree in Chemical Engineering,
Stevens Institute of Technology, Hoboken, New Jersey, 1973
Bachelor of Science Degree in Chemical Engineering,
Taiwan Christian College of Science and Engineering, 1969

CONTINUING EDUCATION

Diploma in Computer Systems and Programming
Computer Learning Center of Tustin (Intensive training in data processing and systems programming, 1982

EMPLOYMENT EXPERIENCE

GENERAL MANAGER,
Chen Laboratories,
Los Alamitos, California (1977–1981)
- managed production, sales, purchasing, and customer relations
- designed programs for accounting, and sales inventory
- supervised production staff
- promoted company to customers
- troubleshot for customer problems
- acted as primary sales representative for products

Sun Soo Chen
Page 2

EMPLOYMENT EXPERIENCE (continued)

PLANT SUPERVISOR,
Theobald Industries,
Kearny, New Jersey (1976–1978)

- supervised staff
- trained chemical operators
- oversaw equipment, operation, production, and quality control
- maintained production on stream troubleshooting

PROGRAMMING EXPERIENCE

Experience on IBM 4331 hardware with 370 software VM/CMS using OS/VSI, DOS/VSE, and POWER/VS. All programs were developed utilizing structured programming design, flowchart/pseudocode, and IPO chart; tested, debugged, and fully documented in the following languages:

- COBOL: Transaction Listing/Error Report, Inventory Report, Inventory Update Exception Report ISAM and SAM Master File, 1-3 Dimensional Table.

- ASSEMBLER: Customer Sales Report, Salesman Sales Report, Commission and Payroll Report, Invoice Register and Mail Labels.

- RGP II: Payroll Deduction Register, Employee Listing, Accounts Receivable, Gross Profit Report, Cash Denomination Report, Airline Passenger Manifest.

- IMS Data Base Management Concept

TRAVEL

Willing to relocate.

* * * REFERENCES AVAILABLE UPON REQUEST * * *

PROBLEMS FOR GROUP DISCUSSION

Study Sun Soo Chen's resume and answer the following questions. Fully explain your answers.

1. Is Sun's education consistent with his career objective?

2. Is Sun's work experience consistent with his career objective?

3. Why has Sun added a subheading called "Continuing Education"?

4. Was Sun's programming experience on-the-job experience?

5. Is his programming experience clearly explained?

6. Would you grant Sun an interview based upon this resume?

7. What seems to have happened to Sun in 1981?

8. How eager to work is Sun? Are there any clues in his resume?

9. What information might Sun wish to add to his resume?

SAMPLE RESUME OF SUN SOO CHEN ONE YEAR LATER

RESUME

Sun Soo Chen
618 Johnston Street
Garden Grove, California 92645
Telephone (714) 992-1138

PROFESSIONAL EXPERIENCE

STARCREST OF CALIFORNIA: January 1983 to Present

As PROGRAMMER/ANALYST, designed, tested, and implemented new selection system driven by parameters in Assembly Language for marketing mailing lists, and developed documentation for the system. Improved sixteen million name selection run time from twenty hours per run to four hours per run. Generated marketing reports. Maintained existing production systems for mailing systems using Assembly, COBOL, PLI, and RPG-II Languages. Debugged production system program. Coordinated adjustments and modifications in marketing mailing system for Marketing Department. Scheduled daily runs. Trained new programmers.

Environment

Experienced on IBM 4331 hardware with 370 software VM/CMS using OS/VSI, and ICCF; DOS/VSE and POWER/VS.

Computer Languages

ASSEMBLER, COBOL, PLI, RPG, CICS, and IMS Data Base Management Concept

CHEN LABORATORIES: May 1979 to October 1981

As GENERAL MANAGER, managed production, sales, purchasing, and customer relations. Supervised production staff. Acted as primary sales representative for products. Set production goals and oversaw product distribution. Handled customer problems and complaints.

THEOBALD INDUSTRIES: June 1976 to June 1978

As PLANT SUPERVISOR, supervised production staff. Trained chemical operators. Oversaw equipment maintenance, and troubleshot for production.

Sun Soo Chen
Page 2

EDUCATION

Diploma, Computer Systems and Programming, Computer Learning Center of Tustin, November 1982. GPA 4.0

M.S., Chemical Engineering, Stevens Institute of Technology, June 1973. GPA 3.0

B.S., Chemical Engineering, Taiwan Christian College of Science and Engineering, June 1969.

* * * REFERENCES WILL BE PROVIDED UPON REQUEST * * *

PROBLEMS FOR GROUP DISCUSSION

Compare Sun Soo Chen's second resume (written one year later) with his first resume. Answer the following questions. Fully explain your answers and be prepared to discuss them.

1. Why do you think he has decided to put experience first and education last in his new resume?

2. What changes has he made in the way in which he presents his educational background?

3. What changes has he made in how he handles his computer experience?

4. What changes has he made in format?

5. Which resume do you think is better if he is applying for a programming position?

_____chapter *8*_____

INTERVIEWING STYLES AND PROCEDURES:

"Selling Your Skills"

_____

Ed Lettau/Photo Researchers, Inc.

INTRODUCTION

There are many different kinds of employment interviews, but generally there are two basic types: the _screening interview_ and the _selection interview_. A _screening_ interview is often based on an employment application. In a screening interview, a personnel clerk or a staff person may review the company's application form you filled out to make sure that you have provided all essential information. Questions will usually require you to provide yes/no answers or give short answers providing specific information. Generally the screening interview is meant to be a check to make sure that the applicants meet minimal requirements before further interviewing is done. In a _selection_ interview you may be interviewed by one or even four or five individuals. These may include a personnel manager or supervisory staff from the section for which you are applying. Questions in a selection interview may ask for specific information or may be more open ended. The more experience you have in analyzing different styles of interviewing, the more flexible and adaptable you will be in dealing with actual interviews.

Every interviewer is different; each has his or her own style. Some are professionally trained, but many are not. In general, however, interviewing styles fall into two broad types: _directive_ and _nondirective_. An interviewer with a directive style will generally ask a number of pointed questions that are aimed at getting specific information. In a directive style interview, the interviewees have less opportunity to control the direction of the interview. In a nondirective interview, on the other hand, the interviewer tends to ask questions that allow the interviewees the opportunity to express themselves more openly.

An interview may be compared to a dance in which the interviewer is supposed to be the lead partner and the interviewee is supposed to be a follower. Most of the time the trick is to adjust yourself to the pace and style set by the interviewer. If the style is directive, you should try to provide concise, accurate information without going on and on. If you have been asked a simple question, try to stick to it rather than trying to provide your whole life story. On the other hand, if you are being interviewed in a nondirective style, try to elaborate by providing specific examples and explanations.

Occasionally you may be interviewed by an inexperienced or poorly trained interviewer. Remember that not everyone is equally skilled in the art of interviewing. Many people who interview do so only now and then as a minor responsibility rather than as their major job. When you are dealing with an unskillful interviewer, it may be necessary for you to redirect the interview. You should make this switch only after you realize that the interviewer's line of questioning is missing important information about you and your background. Just as in a dance in which a lead person fails to lead and it may occasionally become necessary for the other partner to lead, so too in an interview it may become necessary for you to redirect.

VOCABULARY CHECK

Match the following terms with the numbered phrase below that best explains the term or concept. Note: *Only six answers are correct.*

_____ a. directive style

_____ b. nondirective style

_____ c. screening interview

_____ d. selection interview

_____ e. elaborate

_____ f. redirect

1. explain fully
2. a check to see that an applicant meets minimal qualifications
3. the actual process of determining whether the applicant is to be hired
4. asking for specific information, thus narrowing the range of response
5. the ability to change your answer
6. asking for general information, thus broadening the range of response
7. asking for clarification
8. changing the lead

QUESTIONS FOR DISCUSSION

1. What is the difference between a directive style and nondirective style?
2. What is the difference between a screening interview and a selection interview?
3. In what way is an interview similar to dancing?
4. What might the interviewee do if the interviewer is not leading effectively?

QUESTIONING APPROACHES

Directive Style Questions

How would you answer the following questions:

1. Do you drive?
2. How long have you lived in this area?
3. Which do you prefer, books or people?

In a directive style interview you may be asked questions such as these. Question 1 calls for a simple yes or no answer. Question 2 is asking for specific information. Question 3 merely asks you to choose between two choices. All of these questions are limited in scope and limited in how you can respond to them. In a directive style interview the interviewer may not want you to go on and on in an answer to questions such as these. Sometimes questions of this type are called _closed questions_, because the interviewee's options in answering them are closed or limited. Study the following situation.

Situation

The interviewer is trying to determine if the distance from work or the means of transportation are factors that would inhibit the applicant's ability to get to work.

Interviewer: How far do you live from work?

Interviewee: About thirty miles.

Interviewer: Do you drive? (_yes/no question_)

Interviewee: Oh yes, I've been driving since I was sixteen. I can drive any kind of car, truck, motorcycle, or whatever. I can even drive a tractor. If it's got wheels I can drive it.

Here the response to "Do you drive" provides too much information. If the applicant were to apply for a job as a driver, it would be appropriate. The trick is not to do an overkill when it's not necessary. Providing far too much information may signal to the interviewer that you have trouble focusing and that you are easily sidetracked.

On the other hand, sometimes failing to provide enough information also creates a problem. The question may appear to require a short answer or limited response, but the interviewer may expect more explanation. Study the following situation.

Robert A. Isaacs/Photo Researchers, Inc.

Situation

The applicant is applying for a job that will require frequent travel. Some people do not like to travel away from home too often. The interviewer wants to make sure that the interviewee does not mind traveling.

Interviewer: Have you done much traveling in recent years?

Interviewee: A little.

Interviewer: Do you like to travel?

Interviewee: Yes.

Interviewer: (*pause*)

Here the interviewer has asked questions that appear to be narrow in scope but that in actuality require some additional information to strengthen the answer. Providing additional information is called providing _reinforcement_. In the situation above, lack of reinforcement may signal to the interviewer that the interviewee is not really very interested in traveling. The short "yes" answer may signal that the interviewee is only trying to please the interviewer. One difficulty with closed or limited-response questions involves not only how much to say but also how to answer appropriately.

Appropriateness of response is a skill that requires trying to anticipate what the interviewer's intention is, or, in everyday speech, it requires trying to determine what the interviewer is "going for." For example, in the question, "Do you prefer to work alone or with people?" the appropriate answer depends on the nature of the job and on how you actually feel. If you are applying for a job as a lighthouse keeper, you had better say, "I prefer to work alone." Most cases, however, are not so clear-cut. If you are familiar with the nature of the position you are seeking, you will probably have some insight into how to answer. Sometimes even though the question is asked as a closed question, it may be necessary to supply an alternative. In the case of the question, "Do you prefer to work alone or with people?" it may be necessary, depending on the job, to state that you are flexible. Many employers want flexible workers who can adapt to many types of work environments.

As we discussed earlier, sometimes it becomes necessary to redirect an interview when important information is being missed by the interviewer. Imagine that you are being asked only closed questions. As the interview proceeds, you begin to have the feeling that the interviewer is missing some of your strongest points. You have both experience and qualifications that should qualify you for the job, but the interviewer does not seem to be asking the right questions.

What can you do? One strategy is to begin your answer with more information than is being asked for. Remember, you should make this switch only after you realize that important information is being missed.

Situation

The interview has been proceeding for ten minutes and the interviewer has been asking only questions that are narrow in scope. You are getting worried that the interviewer is missing important information about your background and experience.

Interviewer: Have you ever had to supervise? (_yes/no_)

Interviewee: Yes. As a matter of fact, on my last job I was responsible for overseeing six workers. Would you like me to tell you about that? (_redirect_)

Interviewer: All right.

The interviewee now has the opportunity to present essential information.

Nondirective Style Questions

Open-response questions are broader in scope than directive style questions. Rather than asking the interviewees for a simple yes/no answer or asking them to choose among several choices, the interviewer allows the interviewees to provide their own response. Open-response questions give the interviewees more of an opportunity to express themselves than yes/no questions and limited-response questions. Study the following.

1. What did you like most about your previous job?
2. Why did you choose engineering as your major?
3. Tell me about yourself.

Note that "Tell me about yourself" is much more open than "What did you like most about your previous job?"

Irene Springer

Open-response questions are generally used more in a nondirective style interview. Although the nondirective style allows you more flexibility in answering, appropriateness of response still requires you to stay on the topic and to anticipate what the intentions of the interviewer are. In the question, "Tell me about yourself," the request for information is deceptively broad. Probably the interviewer is not interested in hearing every detail about your life. In responding to this question, you would want to discuss strong points in your character as they relate to work. Provide specific examples to demonstrate general qualities that you possess.

QUESTIONS FOR DISCUSSION

1. In a directive style interview are you more likely to be asked open or closed questions? Explain.

2. Explain what reinforcement means.

3. What is meant by appropriateness of response?

4. Would you be more likely to redirect if the interviewer was using open questions or closed questions? Explain.

EXERCISE

For each request for information below, indicate whether the request is open (indicate by writing O) or closed (indicate by writing C).

_____ 1. Why did you leave your last job?

_____ 2. Which do you prefer when you start a new project, a lot of direction or little guidance?

_____ 3. Do you enjoy going to parties?

_____ 4. What goals do you have for the future?

_____ 5. Describe the kind of boss you would like to work for.

_____ 6. Which subject was more difficult for you, English or math?

_____ 7. When you supervise people, how do you try to motivate them?

_____ 8. Can you work under pressure?

_____ 9. Which do you prefer, books or people?

_____ 10. Will you accept $2,000 per month to start?

_____ 11. Do you have any problems with your health?

_____ 12. Will you work overtime?

_____ 13. What kind of salary are you looking for?

_____ 14. Do you drink alcohol?

_____ 15. Tell me about your childhood.

STRATEGIES FOR GETTING MORE INFORMATION

In addition to basic question types there are several strategies an interviewer may use to get information on a deeper level or to clarify statements made by the interviewee. Two of these strategies are *probing for more information*, and *restatement for clarification*.

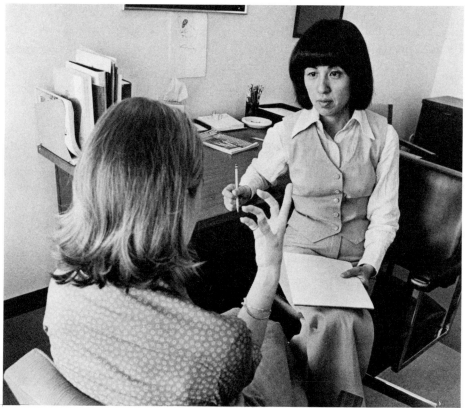

Frank Siteman/Taurus Photos

Probing for More Information

When an interviewer probes, he or she is attempting to find more information about the interviewee's attitude, interests, situations, or experience. Study the following.

Situation

Eduardo is applying for a job requiring some degree of experience in supervising people.

Interviewer: How much supervisory experience have you had? (*limited-response question*)

Eduardo: Three years.

Interviewer: How many people did you supervise? (*limited-response question*)

Eduardo: Four at first, ten later.

Interviewer: Tell me about your responsibilities toward those people. (*probe for more information*)

Eduardo: Well, I was a section chief; it was my job to make daily assignments and to make sure that people were on schedule.

Interviewer: Give me an example of your dealings with the people you supervised on a typical day. (*probe for more information*)

Note that the probes for more information have the same appearance as some of the basic types of questions we have been discussing. The difference between probes for more information and the other question types is based upon the interviewer's desire to get more information through a general line of questioning and desire to get to information on a deeper level. Failure to probe results in a very shallow interview.

Restatement for Clarification

Restatement is a common strategy used by interviewers to try to clarify response (it may also be used to probe). In this strategy the interviewer may merely repeat all or part of what has just been said, or he or she may paraphrase or give a short summary of what has been said. Usually a questioning tone is used, even though the restatement is in statement form. Study the following.

Situation

Toshio is applying for a sales job. The interviewer is interested in knowing more about his ability to handle himself in public.

Interviewer: How often do you entertain people? (*limited-response question*)

Toshio: Oh, my wife and I, we throw parties all the time.

Interviewer: You throw parties ALL THE TIME? (*restatement for clarification*)

In this situation, although the interviewer would like to see some evidence of socializing, she is surprised by Toshio's "all the time." She is signaling that he will need to clarify this with some explanation.

Situation

Kailay is applying for a position as a management trainee. The interviewer is trying to determine her flexibility.

Interviewer: Do you like a variety of tasks throughout the day? (*yes/no question*)

Kailay: Well, not really.

Interviewer: Not really? (*restatement for clarification*)

Here the response has not been one that the interviewer expected. Kailay will have to explain why she does not like variety in her work. It's possible that previously she has done work that was too demanding to allow for flexibility. It may be that her answer was based only on past experience. If so, the interviewer may lead her to see that flexibility can be seen as positive in terms of the position for which she is applying.

Restatement for clarification may be followed by a pause. The pause is often an indication that the interviewer is waiting for you to explain or add more.

VOCABULARY CHECK

Using terminology from the reading above, fill in the blanks below with the correct term.

1. Repeating what someone has said to signal a need for more

   information is called a _____ .

2. Stopping momentarily during a conversation is called a

_____ .

3. Attempting to take the interviewer to a deeper level of explanation is referred to as _____ .

4. Repeating the essence of what someone has said is known as

_____ .

5. An interview in which there is little probing is a

_____ interview.

WHAT MIGHT YOU BE ASKED IN THE INTERVIEW

Because an interview does not follow a script, it is impossible to predict what you will be asked. However, in most interviews you will be asked questions that fall into several broad question types.

Bob David

Questions to establish a rapport. These are friendly questions that are designed to put you at ease. These questions may also be designed to see how well you can handle simple social interaction and how well you present yourself.

Examples

How are you today?

Did you have any trouble finding us?

What do you think of the weather lately?

Would you care for some coffee?

Questions to determine skills and qualifications. These are questions aimed specifically at determining whether or not you can do the job. For these questions it is a good idea to give specific examples that explain your training or education or specific examples of your experience or skills.

Examples

Which courses did you feel were most helpful?

Tell me about your experience.

What did you do on that project?

Can you operate a 1640?

Questions to determine what kind of a person you are. These are designed to determine how well you will get along with other people at work. Once it has been determined that you have the necessary skills or other qualifications, the kind of person you are may sometimes be the most important thing to the interviewer.

Examples

What do you do during your free time?

Tell me about your childhood.

How much and how often do you drink?

Do you enjoy pleasing others?

Questions about how you perceive yourself. These are often asked to determine how realistically you view yourself and to determine whether or not you have strategies for self-improvement. These questions often appear to be in general, but remember that they are often intended to determine what type of employee you will be.

Examples

What do you consider your strong points to be?

What are your greatest weaknesses?

How reliable are you?

Are you an achiever?

Questions about salary. These are often asked to determine whether your expectations are reasonable and whether the organization can afford you. Try to find out what salary ranges are common in your field and what the ranges are for the company where you are applying. _Hint_: It is better to give a range than a specific figure.

Examples

What kind of salary are you looking for?

How much do you expect to earn?

What would we have to pay you?

Questions about your career expectations. These are often asked to determine whether your career goals are reasonable given the position for which you are applying and given what the company can realistically offer you. They may also be designed to determine whether or not you intend to stay with the company if you are hired.

Examples

Where do you expect to be in five years?

What are your career goals?

VOCABULARY CHECK

Match the following terms with the numbered phrase that best explains the term or concept. Note: _Only six answers are correct._

_____ a. rapport

_____ b. skills

_____ c. qualifications

_____ d. self-perception

_____ e. career expectations

_____ f. salary range

1. the most that you can be paid
2. the ideas that you have about yourself
3. the ideas you have about your employment future
4. a comfortable feeling established between people
5. the things you can do
6. the things that indicate you are able to do something
7. the upper and lower limits of what you can be paid
8. what you hope to be able to accomplish in your field of work
9. a way of knowing your own mind better than others can know it

PROBLEMS FOR ANALYSIS AND DISCUSSION

Answering Some Tough Ones

There is no way to predict which questions you will be asked, but questions such as the following often present problems for the interviewee. For each question, try to think what the interviewer may be going for, that is, what he or she is trying to find out. To do this, try to imagine that you are the interviewer asking each question. Why would you ask such a question? Second, try to imagine yourself as the interviewee and try to think how you would answer each question.

1. Tell me about yourself.

2. What is your strongest point?

3. What is your major weak point?

4. Which is more important to you, the money or the job? (What do you think the interviewer is going for?)

5. What was your best subject in college? (What do you think the interviewer is going for?)

PROBLEMS FOR ANALYSIS AND DISCUSSION

Getting through the door for an interview is often half the battle for a job. Sometimes positions are not well advertised, and you may not hear about the position until it is too late. Other times the position is too well advertised and a thousand people seem to be trying to get in the door ahead of you. Any advance information about a job, whether the information comes from formal sources like ads in the newspaper or from informal sources like tips from people you know, will help you get through the door.

Case 1

Ala is a young woman with some educational background and training in computer science. Last night her friend called her and said that the data section where she works may have an opening, but her friend does not have any specific information about the job.

If you were Ala what would you do?

_____ a. Go to the company as soon as possible and ask for an interview.

_____ b. Mail a resume to the company.

_____ c. Ask her friend to try to find out more about the position.

_____ d. Other (Explain your own response.)

Additional Cases

Analyze how you would handle the following situations.

1. You feel that in the near future a local company will probably be hiring engineers. You have just completed a degree in engineering and would like the company to see your resume. As yet, no positions have been formally advertised. Explain what you would do.

2. You have a friend who is a manager for State Insurance Company. You would like him to interview you for a job. How will you approach him on this subject? Explain.

COPING WITH THE UNEXPECTED IN AN INTERVIEW

Interviews generally do not go according to script. Sometimes there are interruptions. Sometimes the interviewer tries to throw you something unexpected to observe how you will deal with it. Sometimes the interviewer wants to know how you can handle stress and may intentionally try to put you in a tough situation. Sometimes you may be interviewed by an inept interviewer whose lack of skill creates problems for you. There's no way you can anticipate what will happen, but practice in dealing with strange and unusual situations can give you experience in learning how to cope with the unexpected.

PROBLEMS FOR ANALYSIS AND DISCUSSION

Case 1

You are going to be interviewed for a position as a sales representative for a large international corporation. You are invited into the office of your interviewer. After introductions are made, you hand the interviewer a copy of your resume. The interviewer takes it from you and then tears it into little pieces and throws it on the floor. Analyze this situation. First explain why you think the interviewer is behaving in such a rude manner. Then explain what you would do.

Case 2

You are being interviewed in a small office in a busy work-oriented company. During the interview, people keep coming in and asking the interviewer questions because he is their supervisor. The interruptions are making it difficult for the interviewer to concentrate on your interview. Should you say anything to the interviewer in this situation? Explain.

Case 3

You are invited into an office for an interview and, to your surprise, you realize that you are facing five interviewers. How would you feel in this situation? Explain.

Case 4

You are invited into an office for a group interview. You will be evaluated along with three other qualified applicants at the same time. How assertive should you be? Explain?

FROM THEORY TO PRACTICE: TRYING IT ON YOUR OWN

Reading about interviewing will provide you with some of the information you need in order to become prepared for an interview. In addition to knowledge, you also need practice. Using the resumes that you prepared in the previous chapter, exchange your resume with that of another member of the class. Study the resume carefully. Imagine that you are the interviewer in an actual interview. What questions will you ask to make sure that you get at the information you need in order to hire this person? Next, exchange roles; now you try being the interviewee and allow the other student to play the role of the interviewer.

Next try holding your interviews in front of the group and allow the other students to observe how well you handle both the role of the interviewee and the role of the interviewer.

As you observe others, you will be evaluating them according to the following skill areas.

Interviewer Skills

- Takes the lead
- Establishes rapport
- Asks a variety of questions
- Probes to get at deeper information
- Seeks clarification when necessary
- Thoroughly analyzes resume
- Allows the interviewee the opportunity to ask questions

Interviewee Skills

- Follows the lead
- Responds to tone of interview set by the interviewer
- Answers appropriately by providing sufficient information
- Seeks clarification when necessary
- Asks appropriate questions
- Redirects when necessary
- Shows a sincere interest in getting the job

Interview Evaluation Form

For each skill below, indicate whether the performance was (+) good, (√) all right, or (−) weak. Make additional comments in the Observer Notes space provided.

INTERVIEWER _____
(name)

_____ Takes the lead

_____ Establishes rapport

_____ Asks a variety of questions

_____ Probes to get at deeper information

_____ Seeks clarification when necessary

_____ Thoroughly analyzes resume

_____ Allows the interviewee the opportunity to ask questions

OBSERVER NOTES:

Interview Evaluation Form

For each skill below, indicate whether the performance was (+) good, (√) all right, (−) weak. Make additional comments in the Observer Notes space provided.

INTERVIEWEE _____
(name)

_____ Follows the lead

_____ Responds to tone of interview set by the interviewer

_____ Answers appropriately by providing sufficient information

_____ Seeks clarification when necessary

_____ Asks appropriate questions

_____ Redirects when necessary

_____ Shows a sincere interest in getting the job

OBSERVER NOTES:

chapter 9

EVALUATIONS:

Being Judged on the Job

Irene Springer

INTRODUCTION

If you work for a large corporation or governmental agency, you will more than likely be reviewed or evaluated by your supervisor or a supervisory team. If you are promoted to a supervisory position, you will probably be asked to review or evaluate the performance of individuals who work under your supervision. The performance review is primarily a means of providing to both management and employees information that they need about the work that is being done and about the responsibilities that have been assigned.

Many organizations require that evaluations of staff performance be made on a regular basis. Some organizations have annual or even biannual reviews of performance. The performance reviews have several purposes. First, they are used to determine whether or not employees are performing adequately in their work. Second, they are sometimes used to determine whether or not employees deserve merit increases for doing outstanding work. Third, they are sometimes used to determine whether or not an employee needs either discipline or coaching. Discipline is occasionally required when an employee has broken organizational rules or procedures. Discipline may involve some form of punishment or denial of promotion to a higher position. Coaching is sometimes used when an employee needs help or training to master a job fully. Coaching often involves assigning an experienced worker to a less experienced worker for the purpose of training and instruction.

It is normal for people to feel uncomfortable about receiving performance reviews. Most people do not like being judged or evaluated by others. Students often feel anxiety about grades; they often seem more concerned about grades than the material they are studying. Conversely, instructors often feel uncomfortable about assigning grades. When one teaches many students for months at a time, it is not easy to be completely objective in grading. Just as a teacher must carefully establish criteria by which students are evaluated, so too a supervisor must carefully follow criteria for evaluating personnel. *Criteria* refers to the standard or measure by which we evaluate the performance of others. If, for example, salespeople are evaluated in terms of how many units they sell, units of sale are the criteria by which they are measured. If, however, they are measured in terms of their amount of sales in dollars (rather than units), then sales dollars becomes the criteria of evaluation.

There are several types of evaluation criteria that are commonly used. One type of measurement is sometimes called a *norm* or *peer reference*. A *norm* is an expected level of performance based upon past experience or based upon taking an average level of performance of a group. Consequently, a *norm reference* is an evaluation in which one is compared with an average or expected level of performance. Similarly, a *peer reference* is

an evaluation in which one is compared with individuals who are working on a similar level. If, for example, five computer salespeople are compared with each other in terms of numbers of computers sold, we may call that comparison a norm or peer reference based upon the number of units (computers) sold.

One of the most common types of evaluation criteria used in evaluations is the _job description_ or _job duty statement_. A job description is an official statement of what the employee is required to do. An accurate job description is essential in helping an employee to understand what the domain of his or her formal responsibilities is.

Another type of performance criteria used in evaluations is _objectives_. Objectives are things that one promises to deliver or produce by a particular date or time. For example, if an employee is responsible for writing monthly project reports, a review by objectives would note whether or not monthly reports are completed on time. If the reports have been completed on time, then that specific job objective has been met. If the objective has been met, then valuable information is being communicated to both management and the employee under review. Both can feel secure in the knowledge that necessary work is being completed on time.

However, if the required reports have not been completed on time, then the reviewer might wish to try to determine the reason why they have not been completed on time. The reviewer might, for example, determine that the employee needs additional training in order to do the assignment properly. In such a case, the reviewer might recommend coaching or additional training for the employee. Or, the reviewer might determine that the employee's overall work load is too great. To correct the deficiency, the reviewer might recommend a change in the objectives for which the employee is responsible.

The reviewer might determine that the employee has failed to meet the objective because he or she has a low sense of commitment or responsibility to the job. In such a case, the reviewer might recommend that corrective action be taken so that the job will be done properly in the future. The corrective action includes a clear statement of what the problem is, allows for the employee to seek clarification about his or her assignment, and then outlines a series of steps that must be taken in order to ensure that the problem is corrected. Corrective action may be taken when discipline is required or when one's work fails to meet expectations of objectives set by the organization. Consequently, periodic follow-up is carried out to check the progress of the employee.

As you can see, a performance review is more than just an evaluation. Actually, it provides an opportunity for formal communication between an employee and supervisor regarding the expectations of the organization and the ability of an employee to meet them.

VOCABULARY CHECK

Match the following terms with the numbered phrase that best explains the term or concept.

_____ a. performance review

_____ b. merit

_____ c. discipline

_____ d. coaching

_____ e. criteria

_____ f. norm reference

_____ g. peer reference

_____ h. job description

_____ i. objectives

_____ j. corrective action

_____ k. follow-up

1. the standard or measure used to evaluate the performance of others

2. things that one promises to produce or deliver

3. check up on one's progress at a later time

4. behavior that deserves a reward

5. a comparison of performance based upon an average level of performance

6. a statement of what one is expected to do in a particular job

7. a critical review of what one has done at work

8. one employee's being assigned to another to help him or her better learn the job

9. an evaluation of performance in which one is compared with other employees who do similar work

10. a form of punishment or denial of promotion used when an employee has broken rules or policies of the organization

11. action taken so that the job will be done better in the future

QUESTIONS FOR DISCUSSION

1. What are some of the reasons why performance reviews are given?

2. What are two types of performance scales that are often used in evaluations?

3. What are some of the possible reasons for poor employee performance?

4. What are some of the positive things a review can recommend?

FACTORS TO LOOK FOR IN EVALUATIONS

What Should Be Evaluated?

What should be evaluated in a performance review? Obviously, an employee should be evaluated in terms of how well he or she is able to do his or her work. However, if one works with the public, or if one must work on team projects with other people, then the employee's attitude or style may also come under evaluation. Cooperation may take on as great an importance as skill and expertise.

In order for employees to understand what is really important in their job, they need a standard against which they are measured. The standard should be written in their job descriptions. The job description should make reference to norms or objectives that are to be met. Progress toward meeting performance norms and objectives should be periodically reviewed and checked. There are two basic types of measures used to check employees' performance: qualitative criteria and quantitative criteria.

Qualitative criteria evaluate the accuracy of work, the quality of work, and other things such as one's sense of responsibility, judgment, knowledge and expertise, and cooperation. Determining qualitative performance is not always easy. If qualitative criteria are to be used, the employee must first have a clear idea of what successful performance requires. Again, this should be outlined in the job description and thoroughly discussed with the employee. The performance evaluation provides an opportunity to review the basic essentials of the job with an employee.

Quantitative criteria include measurables, things that can be counted such as the number of units produced or sold, the number of forms typed, and so on. Keeping track of quantitative performance is generally easier than documenting qualitative performance. Workers can be required to keep performance logs of work done, which can be reviewed by a supervisor or evaluator prior to an evaluation.

Who Should Review an Employee?

Generally the immediate supervisor is the best person to review an employee, for several reasons. First, the immediate supervisor usually has the best understanding of the job; second, he or she usually has been in the best position to observe the daily performance of the employee under review.

Although it is common for employees to fear the "boss," actually one of the important roles of a supervisor is to serve as a bridge between the employee and management. Often management is not in a position to decide which employees should be rewarded or promoted and which ones should be disciplined or coached. Consequently, it is generally best that the immediate supervisor perform this role.

Other approaches are possible, however. Some organizations have expert evaluators or even teams of evaluators come into a department from the outside. In some cases, employees are evaluated by their peers. In universities, for example, it is a common practice for faculty evaluations to be conducted by members of the same department.

Why Should an Evaluation Be Conducted?

Performance evaluations provide an opportunity for communication between the employee and the supervisor about the expectations of the organization and about how well the employee is meeting those expectations. If an employee's level of performance is too low, the reason needs to be determined. As we suggested earlier, the reasons for low performance are not always the fault of an employee. During the performance evaluation the supervisor or the reviewer should probe to determine the reasons for low performance.

In a case where an individual is making adequate progress, the reviewer can discuss ways in which performance can be improved. Consequently, the performance review can serve as a form of interview in which the reviewer attempts to probe for information from the employee that will help to determine ways in which improvement can be made. The interview then becomes a means of motivating the employee. Benefits of improved performance should be explained to the employee. In most jobs there is some form of career ladder or job ladder. That is, successful performance at a lower-level position usually leads to a higher-level position. In order for an employee to feel motivated to work at a higher level of performance, he or she needs to know what the rewards of hard work are.

Many organizations use the performance review as a means of justifying promotions. Promotions to higher levels of responsibility and higher levels of wages are generally based upon merit. The review process then becomes the formal means by which an organization can justify why one individual was promoted rather than another. In the same way, however, organizations can use an evaluation to justify a demotion in which an employee is required to take a lower position than he or she previously had. Demotions are not common, but in the case of an employee who has consistently demonstrated below-average performance, a demotion provides an alternative to firing the employee. In the case of a demotion, the performance interview becomes the formal means of communicating to the employee the specific reasons for the lowering of his or her job status.

VOCABULARY CHECK

Match the following terms with the numbered phrase that best explains the term or concept.

_____ a. qualitative criteria

_____ b. quantitative criteria

_____ c. performance log

_____ d. immediate supervisor

_____ e. expert

_____ f. peers

_____ g. motivation

_____ h. career ladder

_____ i. rewards

_____ j. promotion

_____ k. demotion

_____ l. fire (someone)

1. one who has special training, skill, and knowledge
2. a standard that measures the amount of work done
3. an increase in responsibility and/or salary
4. those who are on a similar level to your level
5. lower level jobs lead to higher level jobs over the years
6. force an employee to leave the job because of low performance or improper conduct
7. a cause or reason that makes a person want to do something
8. what one receives for doing something good
9. a decrease in responsibility and/or salary
10. a standard that measures the characteristics or degrees of performance
11. a written record of work that has been done
12. the person who oversees one's work on a daily or regular basis

QUESTIONS FOR DISCUSSION

1. Explain the difference between qualitative and quantitative measures.
2. Who usually reviews an employee?
3. What are some of the reasons for conducting evaluations?

WHAT EVALUATIONS SHOULD NOT DO

Evaluations Should Not Be Done in a Hasty or Hurried Manner

In order to do a fair evaluation, a supervisor needs to take the time to observe the daily work of the employee. He or she needs to review the job description in advance of the evaluation. A supervisor also needs to take the time to review performance logs if they are used, to compare the amount and quality of performance with those of other workers on a similar level, and to talk to other individuals who work with the employee to get their feedback. If performance is low, the supervisor should attempt to determine the reasons for the low performance before conducting the actual evaluation interview with the employee. Alternatives for corrective action can be considered in advance.

Evaluations Should Not Rate Everyone as Equal or Average

Evaluating everyone as average or equal is unfair to those employees who are performing at a higher level than their peers. It is also unwise to give a low performance an average rating if the low-performing employee is not shown how to improve. In the case of a small department where most employees can easily observe each other, if all the workers get an average evaluation, good workers are likely to feel resentment toward low-performing workers, and low-performing workers are likely to feel that they are not expected to improve. Consequently, the morale of the whole department can go down as well as the performance of individuals.

Irene Springer

Evaluations Should Not Confuse Performance with Personality

A fair evaluation should rate an employee's performance rather than the employee's personality. In the case of a likable employee, it is easy to inflate the evaluation because the employee is friendly and easy to get along with. If a supervisor has had a personality conflict with an employee, however, it is easy for him or her to fall into the trap of using the evaluation as a chance to get even. Most employees are sensitive about such abuses of authority. Consequently, the supervisor needs to make sure that the evaluation is truly evaluating the overall performance of the employee. If a supervisor feels that he or she cannot give an objective evaluation, then arrangements should be made to have someone else do the evaluation.

Evaluations Can Be Positive as Well as Negative

Evaluations need to provide the employee with information about both strengths and weaknesses. When weaknesses are discussed, coaching or counseling should be provided so that the employee is shown how he or she can improve. Although an evaluation interview involves criticism, it should provide constructive criticism from which the employee can benefit. The evaluation can also provide an opportunity to discuss career opportunities, that is, opportunities for advancement.

An Evaluation Should Not Overgeneralize

The issues discussed in a performance evaluation should relate specifically to the job. Comments on the evaluation should not be overgeneralizations. Compare the following:

Specific	*Overgeneralized*
Called in sick 23 days during the past six months. Average for the department was 3 days.	Called in sick too often.
Produced 214 units during the past quarter. Average for the production team was 175.	Works very hard.
Failed to follow production suggestions made by line supervisor on October 15; again refused to cooperate with production supervisor on October 17.	Uncooperative.

As you can see, the more specific the information, the better it is. In cases where there are disputes about one's performance, specific information is useful. Regardless of whether you are being evaluated or are doing the evaluation, documentation is helpful (especially in situations where the evaluation is disputed).

VOCABULARY CHECK

Match the following terms with the numbered phrase below that best explains the term or concept.

_____ a. resentment

_____ b. morale

_____ c. inflate

_____ d. personality conflict

_____ e. get even

_____ f. abuse of authority

_____ g. constructive criticism

_____ h. overgeneralization

_____ i. incident

_____ j. document

1. bad feeling or disagreement based upon different styles of behavior
2. explaining both strengths and weaknesses so that improvement can be made
3. something that happens and attracts attention
4. keep a record of events or things that happen
5. a conclusion made without reference to specific facts
6. spirit, attitude (positive or negative), or temperament of a person or group
7. bad feeling toward someone because of something he or she did to you
8. exaggerate the importance of something more than is necessary or realistic
9. one in a superior position taking advantage of one in a subordinate position

10. intentionally try to harm someone you feel has previously harmed you

PERFORMANCE INTERVIEWS

What are some of the things that can occur in a performance interview? Study the following dialogue from a performance evaluation; pay close attention to the comments in the boxes.

A Positive Interview

The interview has been going on for several minutes. The supervisor began by trying to establish a rapport with the employee. Next she explained that the purpose of the interview is to discuss the progress of the employee toward meeting expectations and regulations established by the company. Now the interview continues by getting into some specific areas.

SUPERVISOR: In terms of the quantity of your work, I feel that you are making reasonable progress to your objectives. All of your reports were completed on time.

> COMMENT: *The supervisor has found something positive about which to praise the employee.*

However, in terms of the quality of your work, I think we can look for a little improvement. Take, for example, the last three reports you turned in. On the report of the 23rd there were several errors in your computation. As for the report of the 27th, you forgot to complete section D, and as far as last week's report is concerned, you failed to complete section F.

> COMMENT: *Now the supervisor is addressing a major issue of concern. Specific information is given to the employee that explains exactly what the problem is.*

Why do think you had these difficulties?

> COMMENT: *The supervisor gives the employee a chance to explain and also is probing to try to determine what the cause of the problem is.*

Mark Mangold/U.S. Census Bureau

EMPLOYEE: Well, I really hate to turn in late work; I guess that I just rushed things a little too much.

> COMMENT: Wisely, the employee doesn't deny the problem but offers a reason as to why the problem exists.

SUPERVISOR: Well, Lisa, we appreciate your efforts to be prompt, but the other departments also need accurate information in the reports.

> COMMENT: The supervisor does not overly criticize the employee but firmly states the reason why better performance is needed.

Do you feel that your work load is too heavy?

> *COMMENT: The supervisor again probes to try to determine the cause.*

EMPLOYEE: Not, really. It's about as heavy as the other people's in the office, I suppose.

> *COMMENT: No special cause is given.*

SUPERVISOR: Do you have any suggestions as to how we can improve upon the situation?

> *COMMENT: No special cause being given, the supervisor now asks an open question to see if the employee can help to find a solution.*

EMPLOYEE: Yes, I think that I should be more careful and try to check the reports over before turning them in.

> *COMMENT: The employee has offered a general solution but needs help in finding a way to improve.*

SUPERVISOR: My suggestion is that we make a checklist for you to review before you turn in each report. Shan has had a little more experience with the reports than you. I'm going to ask her to make a checklist for you to refer to before you turn in your reports. After you have checked them, let her take a look at them to make sure you haven't missed anything. I'm going to check back with her in two weeks to see how you're doing. If you have any questions, you can ask her, or you can feel free to ask me.

> *COMMENT: The supervisor has suggested that guidelines be developed to help the employee, and coaching has been recommended. A positive course has been outlined for improvement, and a positive attitude has been established.*

A Negative Interview

In the case above, we saw a positive evaluation process, but in the next case we will see how things can go wrong. Study the following case and again pay close attention to the comments in the boxes.

Let's look at a slightly different situation with the same employee and the same supervisor. This time, however, the supervisor has not begun by trying to establish a rapport with the employee. The supervisor is unhappy about the performance of the employee and decides to begin with the negative parts of the evaluation.

SUPERVISOR: Lisa, I'm really unhappy with you. You're always late with your reports. What's the matter with you anyway?

> COMMENT: *The supervisor sets a negative tone for the interview and then makes an accusation and asks an accusing question. Note also that no specifics are presented in the accusation.*

EMPLOYEE: Well, it seems that no matter what I do or how hard I work you never like it.

> COMMENT: *Because the supervisor personalized the criticism, the employee has responded on a personal level. Also, because no specifics were given to the employee, the employee now overgeneralizes by saying, "you never like it."*

SUPERVISOR: Lisa, your problem is that you have a bad attitude and you don't care about your work.

> COMMENT: *The supervisor keeps her criticisms on a personal level and continues to avoid any specific areas for analysis.*

EMPLOYEE: My attitude is no worse than that of the rest of the people around here.

> COMMENT: *No progress is being made; the overgeneralization is getting further away from anything related to the specific problem.*

SUPERVISOR: Well, I'm warning you that if your attitude doesn't change pretty soon, you're going to be in real trouble.

> COMMENT: *Abusing the privilege of her authority, the supervisor now makes a threat. No positive course of action can be taken to improve the employee's poor performance because no specific problem other than a bad attitude has been identified. The stage is set for a major personality conflict.*

PROBLEMS FOR ANALYSIS AND DISCUSSION

The following case contains some things that are positive and some that are negative. After studying the dialogue carefully, make brief comments in the comment boxes. Briefly state whether you think the person in the dialogue handled the situation positively or negatively and give a reason for each answer. Be prepared to discuss your answers with the class.

Case 1

Kim, a supervisor, is evaluating Mari, an employee. Kim feels that Mari is a slightly better than average employee. The quantity of her work is 10 percent higher than the office average. The quality of Mari's work has generally been good; there are few errors in her work. In fact, Kim had considered giving Mari a promotion, but Mari has one area where improvement is needed first. Mari's sick leave is 15 percent higher than average for the department. Kim believes that before Mari can be recommended for a promotion, she must prove that she is more reliable and can set a better example for the other workers. Kim has briefly explained the purpose of the evaluation to Mari and has established a friendly but professional tone. Now the evaluation interview continues.

KIM: Mari, I'd like you to know that the company is pleased with your work; you seem to be handling a lot of work. In fact, you're currently doing about 10 percent above average for the department, so we hope you'll keep up the good work.

> COMMENT:

MARI: Thanks, I try to do my fair share of work.

COMMENT:

KIM: In terms of the quality of your work, it usually looks pretty good. In fact, Mrs. Johnson in the Data Department commented to me last week that your work has really improved since you first came here.

COMMENT:

MARI: Well, I'm glad to hear that. By the way—you know that I've been here about one year now and I feel that, given the fact that my work is progressing so well, I should be considered for a raise.

KIM: Mari, your work is good, but we can't possibly give anyone a raise just because he or she does good work.

COMMENT:

MARI: But Fred Jones was just given a raise and he doesn't work any harder than I do. I think I deserve a raise and I have a right to one.

COMMENT:

KIM: I'm sorry, Mari, but Fred's case is different. We aren't considering giving you a raise at this time.

COMMENT:

Now Mari, there's one problem area in your work that we need to discuss.

COMMENT:

MARI: Oh really. So what's the big problem?

COMMENT:

KIM: It's about your being sick so often. In the future we want you to bring in a doctor's note when you return to work.

COMMENT:

MARI: Is this some new policy of the company, or is it only required of me?

COMMENT:

EVALUATION FORMS AND PROCEDURES

Most organizations have some established procedures for performance evaluations. Generally they use standardized *rating forms*, which are official report forms, much like report cards used in schools. On these forms they use a standardized *rating scale*. A rating scale provides general guidelines and definitions of degrees of performance.

Typical Rating Terms

Rating forms often use terms such as the following:

Unacceptable

Complete inability or unwillingness to do assigned work accurately and in sufficient quantity, and to accept routine responsibility.

Poor

Inability or unwillingness to perform work with satisfactory accuracy and/or in satisfactory quantity, and to demonstrate acceptable responsibility.

Satisfactory

Ability and willingness to perform work with acceptable accuracy, maintain a normal or average share of work, and accept normal responsibility.

Above Average

Demonstrated ability and willingness beyond normal or average expectation. Demonstrates a high degree of accuracy, carries an above average work load, and seeks and carries a high degree of responsibility.

Superior

Demonstrates a unique or uncommon ability and willingness to work well beyond expectation. Demonstrates resourcefulness, excellent judgment, and exceptional performance, and seeks out and maintains an exceptional level of responsibility.

Much like a grading system used in school, these rating definitions can be given a numerical weight or a letter grade. For example, a numerical weight can be given to the definitions as follows:

UNSATISFACTORY = 0	ABOVE AVERAGE = 3
POOR = 1	SUPERIOR = 4
SATISFACTORY = 2	

Next these numerical ratings are applied to the various criteria used on the evaluation form. The form usually includes both qualitative and quantitative criteria. Study the following list of evaluation criteria.

Qualitative Criteria

Accuracy (works without errors)
Judgment (considers all facts)
Resourcefulness (needs little help)
Responsibility (needs little supervision)

Quantitative Criteria

Amount (how much produced)

Completeness (finishes work)
Speed (works quickly)

(*Note:* In addition, evaluation rating scales may include information related to tardiness and absenteeism.)

Study the following evaluation form.

SAMPLE EMPLOYEE EVALUATION FORM

EMPLOYEE NAME _____ DATE _____

POSITION/TITLE _____ EVALUATOR _____

DEPARTMENT _____

- -

INSTRUCTIONS: *Fill in the numerical score in the space provided and add brief comments below. 4 = SUPERIOR, 3 = ABOVE AVERAGE, 2 = SATISFACTORY, 1 = POOR, 0 = UNSATISFACTORY*

- -

_____ AMOUNT OF WORK

- -

_____ ACCURACY OF WORK

- -

_____ JUDGMENT

- -

_____ RESPONSIBILITY

- -

_____ DAILY ATTENDANCE

- -
- -

Each employee is required to sign this form to acknowledge that he or she has participated in the evaluation interview and has read this rating form. *Note:* Your signature does not mean that you agree with the rating but merely that you have read it.

- -

EMPLOYEE'S COMMENTS (*Optional*) _____

_____

EMPLOYEE'S SIGNATURE _____ DATE _____

REVIEWER'S SIGNATURE _____ DATE _____

FROM THEORY TO PRACTICE: TRYING IT ON YOUR OWN

Being Reviewed and Conducting Reviews

In the following cases you will be asked to conduct a review or respond to a review during a performance interview. In each case, you will be given a series of facts related to the situation. Be sure to study these facts carefully.

Case 1

SITUATION

You supervise an office of ten people. You are required to conduct a performance review on each employee once each year. Presently you are reviewing Mark Alexander. Mark has been with the company two years. He works as an electronic assembler. Mark learned quickly during his first few months. He was given a raise at the end of his first year. You have the option to give him a raise at this time, but you must justify all raises to the personnel manager who sets the guidelines for raises. According to the personnel manager, an employee must be doing above average work in all categories in order to merit a raise.

FACTS:

- Mark's performance is 5 percent higher than average.
- His work is usually turned in ahead of schedule.
- He was ill three times in the last year and missed six days of work.
- Other employees in the department missed an average of eight days each.
- Mark's work passes quality inspection 97 percent of the time, compared with 93 percent for the department.
- Mark rarely asks for or needs help in his work.
- He will ask for additional work if he finishes his assignment ahead of schedule.
- Mark volunteered to help train a new worker last month.

Instructions: _Fill out a sample employee evaluation form and make comments using the facts above. Compare your ratings with those of the rest of the class and discuss your reasons for giving the ratings._
Will you recommend that Mark get a merit raise? Explain:

Case 2

SITUATION

You have been asked to evaluate Tran Luong. Tran has been doing his current assignment for three months. Tran is a line inspector. His job is to ensure that units on the line are acceptable so that they may be sold. Tran must check the work of thirty workers on the line. Your job has been to oversee Tran and ten other inspectors. Periodically, you double-check Tran's work as well as that of the other inspectors. The position of line inspector is very important. It is more cost effective to catch mistakes early before defective units have left the factory than to have them returned for repair after being purchased. Also, the company is trying to improve its image as a producer of high-quality merchandise. As you prepare to give him his evaluation, consider these facts:

FACTS

- Tran has an accuracy rate of 89 percent. Average for the inspectors is 98 percent.
- Tran is required to turn in daily reports. He usually turns them in late, but you have noticed that he always stays late to work on them.
- Tran has never missed a day at work. Average for the inspectors during the past three months was four days absent. Before his promotion to line inspector, Tran was one of the most productive line workers.
- Tran has had some trouble since his promotion with several line workers. He has had several arguments with three different workers in the past three months.
- You confronted Tran two weeks before about two defective units he had approved as being all right. Tran said, "OK, OK, it's no big deal."

Instructions: *Fill out a sample employee evaluation form and make comments using the facts above. Compare your ratings with those of the rest of the class and discuss your reasons for giving the ratings. Will you recommend that Tran (1) get a merit raise, (2) receive coaching, or (3) get demoted back to line worker. Explain:*

Case 3

On the basis of what you have learned, try to conduct an evaluation interview. Practice the role play first in pairs. Next have several individuals try it in front of the group. Those who are observers should make their comments in the space provided.

SITUATION

One person assumes the role of an employee who is being evaluated, and the other person assumes the role of a supervisor who is doing the evaluation interview. The supervisor defends the scores on the evaluation as given, and the employee raises questions that are of concern.

PERSON A:

You are an employee. You feel that the quantity of your work is about average for the office but that the quality of your work is better than that of most of the other workers. You have been with the company for two years and want to have a promotion. Recently you have had to train three new people in the office, even though they are on the same job classification level that you are on. For this you have not received any special recognition or any extra pay. You hope that your boss is aware of your skills and ability and that you will get a promotion and a raise. (You have received the evaluation below.)

PERSON B:

You are a supervisor who has to evaluate person A. You feel that person A has some strong points such as reliability and good quality of work. However, you feel that person A sometimes talks too much and consequently does not do as much work as could be done. You feel that person A is smart and learns quickly but is not conscientious enough. You feel that in the future person A might be able to get a promotion, but not until his or her productivity increases. (You have given the evaluation below.)

OBSERVER NOTES:

SAMPLE EMPLOYEE EVALUATION FORM

EMPLOYEE NAME _____ DATE _____

POSITION/TITLE _____ EVALUATOR _____

DEPARTMENT _____

- -

INSTRUCTIONS: Fill in the numerical score in the space provided and add brief comments below. 4 = SUPERIOR, 3 = ABOVE AVERAGE, 2 = SATISFACTORY, 1 = POOR, 0 = UNSATISFACTORY

- -

__1__   AMOUNT OF WORK

Produced an average of 15 units per day (dept. average = 24)

__4__   ACCURACY OF WORK

Fewer than 1% errors (average for dept. is 4%): superior quality

__2__   JUDGMENT

Sound judgment in work, but socializes with others during work

__2__   RESPONSIBILITY

Reliable; will work overtime, but won't initiate work on her own

__3__   DAILY ATTENDANCE

Called in sick 4 days in past 6 months (dept. average = 6 days)

- -

Each employee is required to sign this form to acknowledge that he or she has participated in the evaluation interview and has read this rating form. Note: Your signature does not mean that you agree with the rating but merely that you have read it.

- -

EMPLOYEE'S COMMENTS (*Optional*) _____

_____

EMPLOYEE'S SIGNATURE _____ DATE _____

REVIEWER'S SIGNATURE _____ DATE _____

chapter 10

CONFLICT MANAGEMENT:

"What's the Problem?"

AT&T Co. Photo Center

INTRODUCTION

In any employment situation some amount of tension, frustration, or even conflict can be considered normal. There are many types of conflict. Some are related to the nature of the work itself. Sometimes when there is too much work, tension builds and employees begin to take it out on each other even when no one in particular is responsible. All too often, however, conflicts are related not to the work but rather to various social or even cultural factors. Sometimes conflicts are related to breakdowns in communication, but they can also occur when people understand each other very well. If people do not share the same views or goals, conflict may be inevitable no matter how well they communicate. At times employees have personality clashes and fail to get along. Although it is best to resolve conflicts whenever possible, many times conflicts cannot be avoided. When you find yourself in a situation where a conflict is unavoidable, it is best to learn to develop strategies to *manage* it.

VARIOUS TYPES OF CONFLICT

As we saw in the chapter on style and attitude, it is not only *what* we communicate that is important, but also *how* we communicate it. In a multicultural work environment some degree of conflict and misunderstanding is unavoidable. When two people from the same culture meet, they sometimes fail to hit it off together because of differences in style or personality. But when two people from different cultures get together, they sometimes feel uncomfortable because of cultural differences. This is so because values, beliefs, and attitudes in one culture are often very different from those held in another. Some cultural conflicts are also caused because there are different expectations about how people should speak, behave, or make decisions.

Many conflicts can be related to unclear chains of command. Imagine how you might feel if your immediate supervisor had given you one assignment, and a little later his boss, whom you normally do not report to, were to come and ask you to do something else. Actually, in this case, your boss's boss would not have shown proper respect for the normal lines of communication. However, given her position in the organizational hierarchy (two levels above yours), you would still have to exercise care in dealing with the conflict in instructions since both bosses would have more authority than you.

Some conflicts are related to tone and register. They tend to occur more often in telephone communication than in face-to-face communication. When using the telephone, many people are not cautious in monitoring their tone and often express irritation in their voice that they would normally try to conceal when speaking face to face. There may be many reasons for this. Telephone conversation is less personal than face-to-face conversation. Since we cannot get nonverbal feedback from the person we are talking to, we may tend to express our irritation and displeasure more openly when using the telephone. According to an old saying, you can judge the personality of an organization by the switchboard operator. It shows how important tone and register are in minimizing conflict with colleagues, potential customers, or people in other organizations.

VOCABULARY CHECK

Match the following terms with the numbered phrase below that best explains the term or concept.

_____ a. take something out on someone

_____ b. breakdown in communication

_____ c. personality clash

_____ d. resolve

_____ e. manage

_____ f. multicultural

_____ g. hit it off together

_____ h. chain of command

_____ i. immediate supervisor

_____ j. monitor

_____ k. conceal

_____ l. image

1. hierarchy of authority
2. contain or control
3. sudden stop in the flow of communication
4. a person's or an organization's appearance to others
5. pertaining to more than one culture
6. establish a rapport with someone
7. find a solution to something

8. the person one directly reports to at work

9. watch closely

10. blame or attack someone without just cause

11. hide

12. conflict based upon incompatible styles and attitudes

QUESTIONS FOR DISCUSSION

1. What are some of the various types of conflict that can occur at work?

2. What is the difference between managing conflict and resolving conflict?

3. Why is understanding culture important in understanding why some conflicts occur?

4. Why are conflicts more likely to occur in telephone conversations?

PROBLEMS FOR ANALYSIS AND DISCUSSION

In the preceding chapters we looked at various factors that can affect one's ability to work and one's adjustment in the workplace. Sometimes conflicts on the job are specifically related to one of these factors. Below, try to decide which conflict area each case is related to. Choose A, B, C, D, or E from the following list, and put it in the space provided in front of each case. Note: More than one answer is possible.

Conflict Area

A. Misunderstood language function

B. Misunderstood urgency

C. Wrong register or tone

D. Inappropriate style or attitude

E. Ambiguous or conflicting domain

_____ 1. Allen's supervisor, Ms. Nakamura, asked him "how" he was doing on a tough assignment. Allen thought she said "What are you doing?" and said: "I'm working on the assignment. What did you think I was doing?" Ms. Nakamura looked upset.

_____ 2. Ngoc does not have much work to do, but other people in the office are busy. Ngoc keeps interrupting their work. Her boss tells her to get back to work. Ngoc responds: "OK, OK, so what's the big deal?" Her boss becomes angry.

_____ 3. Cesar's supervisor has given him an assignment that is very difficult. Cesar sits for a long time trying to decide how to approach it. His boss asks him how long he's planning to just sit around. Cesar says (sincerely) "About thirty minutes." His boss says: "Quit loafing and get started."

_____ 4. Vanary was given 150 pages to photocopy at 4:15 P.M. The material must be express mailed before 5:00 P.M. As Vanary begins to copy the material, a number of people come to the machine, each with only one or two sheets to copy. Vanary politely allows each person to go ahead of him. When his boss sees him standing in line, he demands to know why the work hasn't been completed.

_____ 5. Nampet supervises five people. One day while at work she has a bad headache. One of her workers comes to her and asks for clarification on a work assignment Nampet gave her a short while earlier. Nampet yells at her and says: "Don't bother me with every little detail. Use your head once in a while and figure it out for yourself." The worker feels very hurt.

Laimute E. Druskis

TIPS FOR MANAGING CONFLICTS

Not all conflicts can be resolved, but some can be managed more effectively. Study the following suggestions which will help you develop strategies for managing conflicts.

Identify and Clarify the Specific Problem

Identify and clarify what the specific problem is about. For example, try to determine if it is related to work issues (those related specifically to the job itself) or whether it is related to the work environment (those related to the social conditions of work). Try to be specific. Is the problem related to behavior, procedure, domain, attitude, or style? When discussing the problem with the other people involved, do not try to cover too many issues at one time.

Consider Your Relationship to Those Involved

How important is the relationship itself? Do you want it to continue? Is it essential that it continue? Consider also what your role is in the relationship and what the role of the other person is. If the relationship is important, you may wish to temper your response or choose your words carefully so that minor conflicts don't become major ones.

Think Before You Speak or React

Consider the possible consequences of what you say before you speak or act. Consider not only what the immediate conflict is about but also its long-term effect upon you and your work environment. Take your time in presenting your position to the other party.

Allow Others Involved to Explain How They See the Problem

Try not to assume that other people involved see the problem in the same way you see it. Allow them to speak for themselves to explain how they see the problem. Do not assume that just because their view is not the same as yours, they are not sincere or not intelligent enough to see the truth.

Discuss the Issue, But Don't Attack the Person

Realize that other people have feelings and a need to save face. Stick to the issue, but try not to attack the person, his or her personality, or physical characteristics. If people see that you are obviously right and that they are obviously wrong, try not to do an overkill once you have proven your point.

If You Can't Resolve It, Try to Manage It

If a problem cannot be resolved, try to determine if it can be managed in such a way that it does not interfere with your work or disrupt the work environment. Remember: Today is the tomorrow you worried about yesterday. How do you think today's problems will look tomorrow?

PROBLEMS FOR ANALYSIS AND DISCUSSION

In each of the following cases, try to determine how the situation could have been handled better. Refer to the previous sections if you are unsure. Briefly explain your answer and be prepared to discuss it with the group.

Case 1

Martina has a disagreement with a co-worker regarding the amount of work that each one has to do. Martina argues that she is doing much more than her fair share of the work. As her co-worker tries to explain her position, Martina walks off in disgust.

How might Martina have handled the situation differently? Explain.

Case 2

Juan has been under a lot of pressure at work recently. His boss has found several mistakes in his work. Juan feels that he has made the mistakes because he has too much work. Juan's boss calls him in and confronts him with another mistake. With anger, Juan replies, "You only criticize me, I've had enough of your criticisms."

Should Juan have handled the situation differently? How so? Explain.

Case 3

Irene is Martha's supervisor. Irene is a difficult person to work for because she is condescending (talks down) to her employees, and she is uncooperative when they need help. On one occasion, when Martha was trying to explain a problem to Irene, Irene refused to listen. Irene told Martha that she was the worst employee she had ever had. Martha exploded and told Irene that she hated Irene and the company and that she was going to quit.

How might both Martha and Irene have handled the situation differently? Explain.

Case 4

Armen works in a small organization with about one hundred employees. Promotions and transfers to other departments are not too frequent. Armen likes this work, but he dislikes his boss's personality. His boss is very egotistical. Whenever Armen completes a project, his boss tries to take credit for it. He minimizes Armen's contribution and work. Armen would like to work for another department or quit and work for another company. But for now there is little chance of a transfer, and also little chance of finding work in another organization because the job market is very tight. Gradually, Armen is becoming apathetic (does not care) about his work. He shows resentment to his boss even on small matters. Others are beginning to notice his poor attitude.

If you were Armen, how would you handle this situation differently? Explain.

LEVELS OF CONFLICT

According to anthropologist Edward Hall, within every culture there are at least three levels of interaction and communication. These are the technical, the formal, and the informal level. On the *technical* level, conflicts can be resolved pretty much by the book. Technicians disagreeing over how to repair electrical equipment can generally refer to manuals to check proper procedures. Consequently, people can usually solve disagreements over technical issues by checking with the proper authority. Even in the case of very technical debates within the scientific community, when authorities disagree, there are fairly strict rules of analysis that are used to handle conflicts. Both data and methods must be analyzed according to scientific procedures, which can be universally used and duplicated. Thus, although individuals involved in technical disputes may feel emotional, conflicts are generally resolved according to rather strict procedures. Cultural conflict is possible on the technical level, but not as likely as it is on the other levels.

Rules of formality for *formal* behavior are different from technical ones in several ways. First, formal rules of behavior are arbitrary, that is, they differ from one culture to another. In formal greetings, Japanese bow and use last names whereas Americans shake hands and often use first names. Historically, such differences have occasionally caused misunderstanding and conflict. For example, when Westerners first began having regular contact with the Chinese Imperial Court, serious misunderstanding occurred over the Chinese practice of the *kowtow* (bowing on hands and knees to show respect to the Emperor). The Westerners felt that the *kowtow* was degrading to the person performing it, and thus they refused to do it. The Chinese, on the other hand, felt that the Westerners' refusal was proof that they really were barbarians who had no respect for authority.

Rules of behavior on the *informal* level are also arbitrary and differ from culture to culture, but there is one basic difference between informal and formal rules: informal rules are often unconscious. In the case of formal greetings, Americans think it strange that Japanese bow, but the difference in cultural behavior is easy to see and we are conscious of it. However, consider how Japanese and Americans use space. For example, consider how close they stand to each other when they greet. Japanese tend to stand a little farther apart than Americans. Unconsciously, this difference may, at least at first, make Japanese and Americans a little uneasy. Without exactly knowing why, a typical American might feel that Japanese are somewhat cold or standoffish, whereas a typical Japanese might feel that Americans are somewhat overly aggressive or even pushy.

As we can see, although tension and conflicts can occur at any level of interaction, they are likely to occur when two cultures have very different rules of formal behavior. Tension is even more likely to occur at an informal level of interaction because many of the informal rules are unconscious.

QUESTIONS FOR DISCUSSION

1. What are the three levels of interaction and communication? Give an example of each.

2. How are disagreements regarding technical issues frequently resolved?

3. Are rules of formal behavior the same from one culture to another? Explain.

4. On which level of interaction are misunderstandings particularly likely to occur?

5. Try to recall intercultural misunderstandings that you may have experienced. What was the specific problem you encountered? On what level did it occur?

ETHNOCENTRISM AND INTERCULTURAL CONFLICT

Tension and conflicts are more likely to occur when people are unfamiliar with other cultures. Many intercultural conflicts are the result of ethnocentrism and of racial or ethnic prejudice.

Laimute E. Druskis

If we say that a person is *ethnocentric*, we mean that the person unconsciously judges people of a different race or ethnic group according to the values of his or her own culture. Take, for example, the case of an American tourist who goes to Mexico and complains that no one understands English. The unconscious assumption of the tourist is that English should be used everywhere in the world. Or, consider an even more extreme case in which the American tourist in Mexico notices that there seems to be a lot of foreigners (meaning Mexicans). Residents in Hawaii are often irritated by mainlander tourists who remark that they are on vacation from the United States.

Closely related to ethnocentrism is the tendency of people from one group to *stereotype* people of a different group. A stereotype is basically an inflated truth. That is, it is a general conclusion based upon some small amount of truth that has been blown all out of proportion or overgeneralized. For example, assume that your friend notices that several businesses in the area have recently been purchased by Chinese immigrants. Your friend then remarks that the Chinese only seem to be interested in business. Here we can see that the small truth is that several businesses have been purchased by Chinese. This fact has been overgeneralized and gives the impression that Chinese only care about business.

Stereotyping involves making a conclusion that is based upon little evidence. The kind of evidence that is often chosen in stereotyping is usually based upon what is called *selective perception*. Selective perception means that people see what they wish to see while ignoring things that they do not wish to see. Often what is ignored is more significant than what is seen. For example, in the case regarding the Chinese businesses, the fact that Chinese are also interested in many other things besides business has selectively been ignored.

In the workplace conflicts that result from ethnocentrism and stereotyping can lead to anger, resentment, or apathy, all of which make life on the job more difficult and reduce productivity. The first step in managing conflicts involving ethnic and/or racial prejudice is to understand how prejudice works. When people are unfamiliar with people of a different group, there is a greater chance that they will react to them in an ethnocentric or even prejudicial way. Many enlightened modern companies send their managers to cultural awareness seminars, where they can be made consciously aware of intercultural differences. Some organizations also sponsor activities wherein employees can get to know one another better. The more everyone becomes aware of the fact that differences are normal, the more conflicts can be minimized.

Occasionally problems may occur wherein you may find yourself on the receiving end of stereotyping or ethnocentric behavior. If this happens, try to treat the problem as a technical matter rather than a personal one. If members of your group or another group are stereotyped, and if you feel that the stereotype needs to be corrected, point out information in a factual way. Try not to get even by stereotyping others. Stick by your rights, but do so in a professional way so that others will be forced to respect you. For example, let's assume that during a break at work someone begins telling ethnic jokes, which you feel are in poor taste because they involve negative stereotypes. If you laugh at the jokes, you appear to approve of that type of humor. If you tell similar jokes about the joke teller's ethnic group, you are retaliating in kind and perpetuating the problem. If you don't laugh, others may realize that their humor is in poor taste. It's possible that you may even have an opportunity to explain your feelings regarding why you choose to avoid ethnic humor.

The most extreme form of ethnocentrism is called *racism*. Racism is based upon the belief that some races are superior to others. Although the concept of race was popular in the nineteenth century and earlier part of this century, it is now discredited and not used by many scientists. Racists (those who practice racism) sometimes directly criticize or attack their opponents. Name calling is a common tactic used by racists, but sometimes they resort to more extreme forms of attack or even violence. If you feel that you are being victimized by racists, you should discuss the matter with your supervisor or personnel director. Within your locality, there is typically a human relations board or commission that monitors racism within the community.

VOCABULARY CHECK

Match the following terms with the numbered phrase that best explains the term or concept. Only eight answers are correct.

_____ a. ethnocentrism

_____ b. prejudice

_____ c. assumption

_____ d. mainlander

_____ e. to stereotype

_____ f. blow all out of proportion

_____ g. selective perception

_____ h. enlightened

1. to overgeneralize
2. something taken for granted without evidence
3. exaggerate
4. get revenge
5. one who lives in the continental United States
6. prejudging based upon a bias
7. emotional belief that one's country, race, or ethnic group is superior
8. informed, knowledgeable
9. reduce in importance
10. a view based upon seeing what one wishes to see and ignoring what one does not wish to see

QUESTIONS FOR DISCUSSION

1. What is meant by ethnocentrism?
2. Define prejudice.
3. What is a stereotype?
4. Give an example of a stereotype that is not found in the text.
5. What are some of the negative results that can come from stereotyping and prejudice?

6. What are some companies trying to do about these problems?

7. What is racism and what should be done about it?

8. Do you feel that you have ever encountered prejudice? Explain.

PROBLEMS FOR ANALYSIS AND DISCUSSION

Case 1

Intercultural tension at work is often felt on the informal level of communication and interaction. Foreigners often feel uncomfortable with jokes and the American sense of humor. To get a joke or understand the humor of a people requires more than a basic knowledge of the language. It also requires knowledge of their cultural psychology and values. The following case was related to us by a young man who had lost his first job in the United States because of a misunderstanding with his boss. It shows in an extreme case what can happen when one fails to have a strategy for dealing with informal misunderstanding.

> When I first came to this country, my English was limited. I got a job in which I had to work closely with my boss. My boss was always telling jokes, but I usually didn't laugh because my English wasn't so good and I couldn't usually catch the meaning. After several weeks he told me that he thought I was unfriendly and had a poor sense of humor. I became pretty nervous around him. I never knew when he was joking or when he was serious. I decided that I had better laugh and smile a lot so I started laughing and smiling all the time. A few weeks later he called me into his office and told me that I was fired. He said he thought that I must be crazy because I seemed to think that everything was funny.

Obviously, this unfortunate fellow's strategy failed to solve the problem. If you were in his situation, how would you try to handle the situation differently? Briefly explain, then discuss your answer with the group.

Case 2

In some cultures "saving face" is important; that is, it is important not to admit a weakness in public. In a work situation, when you wish to appear competent, sometimes it is easy to feel conflict between saving face and trying to appear competent. Consider the following case.

Luong has been working at a company for several months. He has successfully completed a training program and has received a good preliminary evaluation. He is anxious to gain responsibility and to show that he can do a good job. Mrs. Williams, his supervisor, gives him an important assignment. She tells him that if he has any questions he should feel free to ask for help. As his work progresses, he runs into a problem that he does not know how to solve. He decides that rather than ask for help, he will try to cover up or hide the problem because he wants it to appear that he can handle it.

If you were Luong, what would you do in the same situation? Briefly explain your answer and be prepared to discuss it with the group.

FROM THEORY TO PRACTICE: TRYING IT ON YOUR OWN

Laimute E. Druskis

In order to try out what you have learned, practice the following role-playing situations either in small groups or in front of the group. Those observing should comment on how effectively those in the role-playing exercise perform. Observers should make notes in the space provided.

Situation 1

Orlando works for an international company. He is married and has two children. His company wants to send him overseas for twelve months to help set up a new office. In this situation the conflict is between family (personal domain) and company. Orlando will not be able to take his family. In order to make the trip seem worthwhile, he will need to negotiate an increase in salary or a bonus. Orlando's supervisor will need to try to keep the increase in salary or the bonus within reasonable limits.

PERSON A:

Assume the role of Orlando. Try to explain why you feel you need more money in order to go overseas.

PERSON B:

Assume the role of Orlando's supervisor. Be willing to compromise but also be reasonable in making the compromise.

OBSERVER NOTES:

Situation 2

Kazumi works in an office with three other people. She has a deadline to meet, and the other people in the office are talking loudly and joking. Kazumi asked them to be quiet twenty minutes ago. They were quiet for about five minutes, but gradually the noise has started up again. Technically, the others are at fault. However, if Kazumi is to remain on good terms with her co-workers, she must try to do three things: First, she must defend her right to have a quiet place to work. Second, she must make her point in such a way that her co-workers do not think she is trying to act superior to them. Third, she must try to impress the seriousness of the situation on them. Several strategies are open to her: She can make the same request again (this may only lead to the same result as before). She can deal with them as a group. She can try an individual approach. She can get very angry. Possibly she can request help. Regardless of her approach, she will need to give reasons and to choose an appropriate style, given the urgency and her status, with the objective of getting her work done while not offending.

Try this exercise first with a group that is somewhat cooperative, and then with a group that is less cooperative.

PERSON A:

Assume the role of Kazumi.

PERSON B:

Assume the role of a co-worker who is talking and joking with person C and person D.

PERSON C:

Assume the role of a co-worker who is talking and joking with person B and person D.

PERSON D:

Assume the role of a co-worker who is talking and joking with person B and person C.

OBSERVER NOTES:

Situation 3

Mehdi has been given more work than he can handle. He has been working overtime every night, but still he cannot finish his work. He needs to have a conference with his boss to discuss the problem. Mehdi's boss also has been working overtime and cannot finish all of his work. The important thing for each person to do in this case is clearly state his problem and needs. Mehdi's boss has no immediate solution to the problem, but the situation may improve within five or six weeks.

PERSON A:

Assume the role of Mehdi.

PERSON B:

Assume the role of Mehdi's boss.

OBSERVER NOTES:

Situation 4

Mikai is on a lunch break in the company cafeteria. She is eating lunch with several co-workers. While she is eating lunch, a person whom she does not know very well (sitting at the table next to hers) begins making negative remarks about people of Mikai's ethnic group. Several people at the opposite table begin to laugh. Mikai does not know what to do. She and her co-workers wait until the others leave and then begin to discuss the situation. Mikai wants to know how her co-workers feel about what has happened, and she wants their advice on what she should do in future situations.

PERSON A:

Assume the role of Mikai.

PERSON B:

Assume the role of Mikai's co-worker, and try to give her some advice.

PERSON C:

Assume the role of Mikai's co-worker, and try to give her some advice.

OBSERVER NOTES:

DATE DUE